Visions of China
Stories from Macau

Visions of China
Stories from Macau

Selection, introduction and translation by
David Brookshaw

A joint publication by

GÁVEA-BROWN and 香港大學出版社
PROVIDENCE, RHODE ISLAND   HONG KONG UNIVERSITY PRESS

Cover by António Conceição Júnior
www.arscives.com
© 2002 Gávea-Brown Publications, and David Brookshaw
Library of Congress Control Number: 2002 141121
All rights reserved. No portion of this publication may be reproduced or transmitted in any form or by any means, electronic or mechanical including photocopy, recording or any information storage or retrieval system, without prior permission in writing from the publishers, Gávea-Brown or Hong Kong University Press.

Published by Gávea-Brown Publications
 Department of Portuguese and Brazilian Studies
 Box O, Brown University
 Providence, RI 02912, USA

Distributed by Luso-Brazilian Books
 538 State Street
 Brooklyn, New York 11217, USA

ISBN 0-943722-29-2
 Secure On-Line Ordering:
 www.brown.edu/Departments/Portuguese_Brazilian_Studies/

In Asia, Australia and New Zealand

Published by Hong Kong University Press
 14/F Hing Wai Centre
 7 Tin Wan Praya Road
 Aberdeen, Hong Kong

ISBN 962-209-592-5
 Secure On-line Ordering: www.hkupress.org

This publication was sponsored in part by the Instituto Português do Oriente, Macau, and the Instituto Camões, Lisbon, Portugal.

To
Celeste Gom Sheng and
Natasha Mei Sheng

TABLE OF CONTENTS

Introduction — 11

Deolinda da Conceição — 21
Cheongsam — 23
An act of charity — 37
A conflict of feelings — 42
The suffering of Lin Fong — 47
The jade ring — 51
The model — 56

Henrique de Senna Fernandes — 61
Tea with essence of cherry — 63
Candy — 97

Maria Ondina Braga — 153
The mad woman — 155
The lepers — 162

The pedicab driver	169
Racial hatred	176
The child of the sun	184

Fernanda Dias — 191

The watermelon	193
The room	199
Tenants	204
Daydream at Hac-Sá	210
The last supper	214

INTRODUCTION

A quarter of a century after the 1974 revolution, which overthrew the country's fifty-year old dictatorship, ushering in a period of decolonisation and democratisation, Portugal relinquished its last remaining colonial outpost, Macau, in southern China. Like its much larger neighbour, Hong Kong, forty miles away across the estuary of the Pearl River, Macau has become a special administrative region of China, its autonomy and way of life guaranteed for a further fifty years. This minute territory of 16 square miles comprises the city and peninsula that gave it its name, and the two outlying islands of Taipa and Coloane, joined to it by bridge and causeway[1]. Prior to 1999, Macau had long since ceased to be a colony in anything but name, for most administrative decisions deliberately avoided confrontation with Beijing, whose influence in the enclave had grown considerably since the 1960s. The vast majority of its inhabitants speak Cantonese, originating as they do from the hinterland of Guangdong, the province where Macau is situated. For most of the twentieth century, there was a more or less continuous inflow of refugees from other parts of China, fleeing civil war, the Japanese invasion, and later the communist revolution, to find safety in the enclave. This 'internal' diaspora served to reinforce a tendency that had been evident since the end of the nineteenth century, namely, the steady emergence of a Chinese commercial elite which counted among its number some of the territory's wealthiest inhabitants.

Comparisons with Hong Kong are, of course, entirely appropriate in this respect, but in other ways Macau was very different from its brash 'British' neighbour. For one thing, it was a much older settlement, having been first settled by Portuguese traders and adventurers in the 1550s, with the agreement of the Chinese authorities. Secondly, its pattern of settlement and consequent social and cultural *mores* reflected a peculiarly Portuguese colonial tradition. The first settlers were, for the most part, lone Portuguese men, who brought with them women from other imperial or commercial entrepots, such as Malacca, Goa, and even Nagasaki and Timor. Later mixture with the local Chinese produced, over the centuries, a Eurasian population, which came to bridge the gap between Portuguese administrators and the Chinese authorities and trading community, serving as interpreters, and staffing the local civil service. The Macanese, as they came to be called, identified themselves as Catholic and Portuguese speaking, even though the language of the home, certainly up until the nineteenth century, was a Creole known as 'Patuá', which had certain affiliations with the 'Papiá Kristang' of Malacca. Patuá was descended from the late medieval Portuguese of the navigators, along with lexical and syntactical characteristics derived from local languages. Most Macanese also spoke more or less fluent Cantonese, even though few of them could write Chinese characters. By the time Portugal handed Macau over to China on 20 December 1999, some four hundred and fifty years after its foundation, this mixed group numbered approximately twelve thousand out of a total population of a little over four hundred thousand.

On the other hand, because of limited employment opportunities in Macau and the various crises that had afflicted the territory over the years, the Macanese had produced their own diaspora in other parts of the world. During the late nineteenth and early twentieth centuries, they had spread to the international settlement at Shanghai and to Hong Kong, and then later to Australia, Canada and California (significantly a major destination for both Chinese and Portuguese emigrants), not to mention Brazil and Portugal[2]. It is the existence of this unique frontier population, coupled with the long and generally unobtrusive Portuguese presence in Macau that has given this new autonomous region of China its distinct characteristics.

It is impossible to talk of a Portuguese literary presence in Macau without referring to two poets whose names are inextricably linked to the city. Luís de Camões probably spent a brief period of exile there shortly after the city had been founded, although the rationale for his presence there is essentially a legendary one, symbolized by the nineteenth-century bust of the poet situated in the rocky outcrop of what is now a public garden, the 'Jardim Camões', where tradition has it, he sat and wrote his epic poem, *Os Lusíadas*. The second poet, Camilo Pessanha, lived there for thirty two years as a teacher and lawyer, wrote essays on Chinese civilization and culture, and died in 1926 from the effects of opium addiction. He lies buried in the city's main cemetery. In the centuries between these two figures, and in more recent years, Macau and China have been evoked by other Portuguese writers who either visited the city or made their careers there, or quite simply spent some years in the territory before moving on. The stories in this anthology not only represent a cross-section of the shorter fiction in Portuguese produced in Macau over the last fifty years, but some of them evoke a historical period which was crucial to this tiny former Portuguese outpost. Portugal's neutrality during the Second World War ensured that Macau was saved from Japanese occupation, which meant too that it became a place of refuge. The war years became engraved in the memories of those who lived through them as a time of trauma and endurance, hunger and hardship. In this respect, it is significant that an entire floor of the 'Museu de Macau' (Museum of Macau) is dedicated to the city during the war years, thus emphasizing their role in reinforcing the city's 'siege culture'.

The stories of Deolinda da Conceição and Henrique de Senna Fernandes, both Macanese writers who experienced those war years, are set at least partially against the background of the Japanese occupation of China and Macau's beleaguered and somewhat vulnerable independent status between 1943 and 1945. Deolinda was a journalist who experienced at first hand the brutality of war, having lived in Shanghai during the Japanese occupation, where she was briefly interned in a concentration camp. In Macau after the war, she worked as a journalist on the main Portuguese-language newspaper, *Notícias de Macau*, where she ran the women's page and also published editorials, chronicles and some of her stories. Her only published collection of short stories came out in Portugal in 1956, a year before her premature death, under the title, *Cheong-Sam, A Cabaia*. The title story of the collection, 'Cheongsam', which features in this anthology, and 'A conflict of feelings', both focus on a theme that was of particular concern to Deolinda, namely, the conflict (often seen as a conflict of loyalty) between the aspirations of western educated women and the expectations placed upon them within traditional Chinese marriage. In the first story, reassertion of independence on the part of the female protagonist has tragic consequences, brought on in part by the hardship and brutality of war, although the exemplary nature of the tale invites the reader to reflect on who was at fault: the wife, the husband, or war itself. In the second story, the woman's choice of freedom, albeit as a concerned mother, leads to a positive and hopeful outcome.

As a Macanese, Deolinda da Conceição straddled the division between east and west, which was why she was particularly sensitive to the position of the mestizo within a hierarchical colonial society. In 'An act of charity', a young man of mixed parentage prepares to leave Macau for Portugal to continue his studies, while he ponders on the shame of his illegitimacy and the malice of his friends and acquaintances. Yet our sympathy is directed towards the figure of the Chinese mother, who emerges from the crowd and is publicly rejected by her offspring, for we know that the woman who gave him life will, like so many in her position, in all probability be abandoned by her Portuguese 'husband', now that the embodiment of the link between them has gone. A similar predicament is described in 'The suffering of Lin Fong', but here, the father of the forsaken woman's unborn child is a soldier, suddenly recalled to Portugal when his battalion leaves. As in 'Cheongsam', the female is punished for turning her back on her own people and placing her misguided trust in a foreigner, but Deolinda suggests that Lin Fong's romantic hope was a response to grinding poverty.

The promise of love as an antidote to poverty and neglect is also the theme of 'The jade ring', in which a young servant girl allows herself to be seduced by an artist, and finds out too late that she has become a concubine rather than a choice for a wife. The problem seems to be that those in flight from social oppression invest their aspirations also in the superficial symbols of that wealth, in this case an unhealthy attraction for a jade ring. The tragic outcome is seen to originate in this, rather than in the legitimate struggle to overcome adversity. The dividing line between women's struggle to be independent and the accumulation of riches is narrow and inherently treacherous. Many of Deolinda's sad characters fall foul of it. Yet the author's underlying message seems to be that the importance of life lies in what one does rather than in how outwardly successful one is, and this is the theme of 'The model', the fifth story by this author to feature here.

The only surviving literary figure of the generation of Macanese intellectuals which emerged after the war, is Henrique de Senna Fernandes, a former teacher and lawyer, and author of two novels, *Amor e Dedinhos de Pé* (1986) and *A Trança Feiticeira* (1993), as well as two collections of shorter fiction. Fernandes is the only writer to concentrate almost exclusively on the inner world of the Macanese, in stories that seek to evoke the customs and society of the 'Christian' city in the early part of the century, and its relationship with the 'Chinese' quarter. Fernandes is essentially a romantic, whose literary models lie in Portuguese novelists of the nineteenth century such as Júlio Dinis. Yet unwittingly perhaps, his stories are also compatible with the rich popular cultural tradition in China in so far as he is a master of the happy ending. It is no coincidence, for example, that his novel, *A Trança Feiticeira*, which recounts the romance between a young Macanese boy and a Chinese water carrier, was turned into a successful film and shown in China. 'Tea with essence of cherry' is taken from his collection of stories entitled *Nam-Van* (1978), and in its vision of Macau and the interface between its 'oriental Portuguese' inhabitants and the 'native' Chinese, as well as in its period setting, is representative of Fernandes' other fiction. Its happy ending, in which its orphan hero and heroine, Maurício and Yao-Man, after much hardship, come together in happy marriage, foreshadows the outcomes of his two later novels in suggesting the emergence of a new, more liberal Macau, in which the city's Portuguese and Chinese traditions were somehow harmonized through the romantic trope of true love.

In 'Candy', also originally published in *Nam Van*, Fernandes touches on the theme of the Macanese diaspora. The tale is developed by means of flashbacks, as two former lovers encounter each other by chance after a period of twenty four years. In a well crafted story, set over a day in Hong Kong in 1970, the recollections of the two main characters – Candy, a Hong Kong Portuguese, and a nameless Macanese migrant in Brazil - range over the war years when they had an affair, leading up to a dramatic climax in which the unexpected is revealed. Candy, the female, rejected her Eurasian Macanese roots when the war ended, in favour of a good marriage to a Hong Kong Englishman. As in some of the stories of Deolinda da Conceição, we are not sure whether Candy's current feeling of alienation from her family, including her 'British' offspring, is punishment for aspiring to wealth, or whether her aspirations were justified by her experience of poverty and humiliation in Hong Kong after the Japanese invasion and in Macau as a refugee. Whatever the case, and the author appears ambivalent in his portrayal of the unfolding recollections of his protagonists, 'Candy' is a story that evokes the vulnerability of the Macanese in the diaspora, and the pressures on them to assimilate the values of their hosts. Unlike the Fernandes prototype, the 'orphan' lovers are not destined to end up together, but are divided by history and the struggle for survival.

Maria Ondina Braga and Fernanda Dias are both writers from Portugal, whose residence in Macau over a number of years was to prove a determining influence on their work. Some four hundred years after Camões left for India, Maria Ondina set off on another epic journey during which she spent time as a teacher at convent schools in Angola, Goa and Macau. Her departure from Angola was hastened by the nationalist uprising of 1961. Similarly, her stay in Goa was curtailed by the Indian invasion of the same year. It was in the aftermath of the fall of Portugal's Indian enclaves that she arrived in Macau, where she stayed until 1966. Stemming from her experience there, she published *A China Fica ao Lado* (1968), a collection of stories that won her critical acclaim in Portugal. Since then she has written further works inspired by her experience of China, notably, *Angústia em Pequim* (1984), a collection of essays and impressions based on a spell at the University of Beijing as a teacher of Portuguese in the early 1980s, and *Nocturno em Macau* (1991), a novel set once again in the city she had known thirty years before. The Macau Maria Ondina encountered in the 1960s was similar to that evoked by Deolinda da Conceição, in the sense that it was a city with an expanding population of refugees from the various upheavals experienced by Maoist China, and which would culminate in the Cultural Revolution. It is, for example, no coincidence that four of the stories included in this anthology refer either directly or indirectly to problems of exile and displacement. For the rest, Maria Ondina adopts the stance of a fascinated observer, whose vision of Chinese difference, or 'otherness', is to some extent informed by the magical realism of the 1960s.

The Macau of Fernanda Dias, a graphic art teacher and engraver, with two volumes of poetry published, and one collection of short stories, *Dias da Prosperidade* (1998), is very different from the city that was home to Maria Ondina Braga some forty years ago. Her stories are set against the background of the transition years beginning in the 1980s, when the relatively small, provincial town experienced a construction boom which transformed its skyline, making it more like Hong Kong. Fernanda Dias' Macau is a city of towering apartment blocks and urban anonymity in 'Tenants' and 'The room'. Gone too are the essentially colonial social relationships, for some of these stories depict the emotional involvement between European female and non-European male, and the negotiations of identity that have to be made to seek to understand and accommodate an unfamiliar culture at an intensely personal level, and within an urban, cosmopolitan environment. Compare, for example, the adjustments that have to be made by the European female in a story like 'The watermelon' or 'Tenants', with Maria Ondina's far more oblique and abstract rendering of the relationship between a European woman and a Chinese man in 'The child of the sun'.

The internationalisation of Macau, with the corresponding decrease in Portuguese influence is suggested in the tale, 'Daydream at Hac-Sá'. For the first time, too, since the days of Deolinda da Conceição, the frontier is open again, and the foreign residents of Macau can travel within China. It is the greater familiarity with the China beyond the border that distinguishes the fiction of Fernanda Dias from the stories of

Maria Ondina Braga. The younger writer witnesses the uncharacteristic modernity of the new, post-Mao China, viewed with bewilderment and some distaste in, say, 'The watermelon'. Macau, for all its redevelopment, becomes for her the symbol of an edenic past. In this respect, the last tale in the collection, 'The last supper', is not only a vignette on the loss of innocence of a lovelorn adolescent schoolgirl for one of her teachers, but it is something of a lament for the possible end of a paradise – the unique cultural identity of Macau and its Luso-Chinese heritage.

I should like to thank Fernanda Dias and Henrique de Senna Fernandes, in Macau, and Maria Ondina Braga, currently living in Braga, for giving me their permission to publish translations of their stories. Similarly, I should like to express my gratitude to António Conceição Júnior in Macau and Dr. Rui Alves in Lisbon, for allowing me to include the work of their mother, Deolinda da Conceição, in this anthology. It was particularly kind of António Conceição Júnior to agree to design the cover of this book at short notice. I am also grateful to Tereza Sena, formerly of the Instituto Cultural de Macau, for putting me in touch with two of the authors, as well as for giving me a copy of her CD-Rom, 'Macau nas Palavras' during my visit to Macau in 1999. I have found it most useful. Equally, I should like to signal my gratitude to Ana Paula Laborinho, Director of the Instituto Português do Oriente, for her welcome on that same visit, and for her interest in my work. A hearty thanks too to John Kinsella, at Maynooth, a colleague and friend of many years, for suggesting I approach Gávea-Brown with this project, to Onésimo Almeida for agreeing to take it on board, and to Alice Clemente for her care and expertise in overseeing the edition. Last but not least, I should like to thank Jane Camens, Director of the Hong Kong International Library Festival, for her help in successfully launching this project.

David Brookshaw
Bristol, England, June 2001

The original stories in Portuguese:
Deolinda da Conceição, 'Cheong-Sam', 'A esmola', 'Conflito de sentimentos', 'O calvário de Lin Fong', 'O modelo', 'O anel de jade', from *Cheong-Sam – A Cabaia*, 4th ed. (Macau: Instituto Cultural de Macau/Instituto Português do Oriente, 1995).

Henrique de Senna Fernandes, 'Chá com essência de cereja', 'Candy', from *Nam Van – Contos de Macau*, 2nd ed. (Macau: Instituto Cultural de Macau, 1997).

Maria Ondina Braga, 'A doida', 'Os lázaros', 'O homem do *sam-un-chê*', 'Ódio de raça', 'O filho do sol', from *A China Fica ao Lado*, 2nd ed. (Lisbon: Livraria Bertrand, 1974).

Fernanda Dias, 'Sai-Kuá', 'Dias do Beco da Prosperidade', 'Inquilinos do pátio', 'Devaneio em Hac-Sá', 'O ultimo chá gordo', from *Dias da Prosperidade* (Macau: Instituto Cultural de Macau/Instituto Português do Oriente, 1998).

---

[1] Macau is the Portuguese name for the territory, derived from the name of the goddess A-Má worshipped by the local fishing community resident around her temple when the Portuguese arrived. The Chinese name for Macau is Ou Mun.

[2] For an excellent study on the Macanese, see, João de Pina Cabral and Nelson Lourenço, *Em Terra de Tufões: Dinâmicas da Etnicidade Macaense* (Macau: Instituto Cultural de Macau, 1993).

DEOLINDA DA CONCEIÇÃO

Born in Macau in 1913, she was a teacher, translator and journalist who lived in Hong Kong and Shanghai, where she was briefly interned by the Japanese during the occupation of the 1940s. After the end of World War II, she worked for the newspaper, *Notícias de Macau*, where she ran the women's supplement and published editorials and some stories. Her only collection of short stories, *Cheong-Sam – A Cabaia*, was first published in Lisbon in 1956, and has since been translated into Chinese. She died in Hong Kong in 1957.

CHEONGSAM

The scream that shattered the silence of night had come from the cell containing the man who, some hours before, had listened, impassive and serene, to the judge sentencing him to life imprisonment.

The guards rushed forward and found him, with vacant expression, staring fixedly at a wall, upon which the shadows of a nearby tree formed strange figures in grotesque positions, driven by the wind battering its branches.

"Get to sleep, A-Chung, and stop worrying about such things. Are you scared of shadows, then?" Asked one of the guards.

As if summoned to his senses after some awful nightmare, the prisoner looked around him and murmured breathlessly:

"I'm sorry, it was nothing, or rather, it was a bad dream. But if it's possible, I'd like to move to another cell. That tree is making me nervous with its shadows."

"Okay, okay, we'll see what we can do tomorrow, because

we can't do anything about it now. Get to sleep and don't bother us anymore. And if you can't sleep, at least get some rest and let the others sleep."

A-Chung calmed down and lay on his cot once again, his hand raised in a gesture of polite thanks. Later, he began to stare wide eyed at the ceiling, but then once again, a cry lodged in his dry throat, a low cry, as if stifled at birth.

The guards came and found him pacing quickly up and down, and mumbling to himself repeatedly

"Take that cheongsam away, tear it up, throw it in the fire. It's got a curse, it's laughing at me, it's alive, it's got her life in it… the one I killed. Ah! She's dead, truly dead, and this is how she gets her revenge, persecuting me with her cheongsam…, but I'm going to tear it up, rip it to pieces, just as I did to her."

"Be quiet, A-Chung, and calm down. Can't you see there's no cheongsam here? Have you gone crazy, man? Get to sleep, and we'll talk tomorrow. But don't disturb people now. The other prisoners need to sleep, if only you'll let them."

A-Chung's clasping hands buried themselves nervously in his hair, and he walked towards the darkened corner of the cell where his cot was. He lowered himself onto the wooden boards, and lay down stiffly, his eyes closed, his body taught and twitching nervously.

Little by little, he calmed down, and silence returned to the gaol, until, at daybreak, it filled with a noise peculiar to prisons, of hundreds of men getting ready for their daily tasks.

Only A-Chung remained motionless, gazing vacantly, head in

hands, as if he were trying to control the thoughts that kept coming to him, causing him time and time again to re-live all the dramatic events of his life.

A strange, and at times seemingly convulsed smile hovered on his half open lips.

He was thirty-two years old and life weighed on his soul like a dark cloud.

Soon, he would be banished into exile, alone, without the comfort of a single friend. Never again would he set eyes on the innocent faces of his three children, cast into orphanhood by a cruel fate. If he suffered now, it was for their sakes; so young were they that they barely understood what life had in store for them.

What a cursed war! A cursed war, that had taken everything away from him and turned him into a criminal, a murderer, a heartless father, a man incapable of rational thought.

Then, as if surprised by his own reaction, he jumped up and went and leaned by the window.

His fate had been decided and that was it. He would leave. His tears would water the land destined to sustain him for the rest of his life, and he would stifle his feelings. His children, his children were no longer his and maybe his cruel fate might prove a blessing to them. They shouldn't have to suffer the consequences of his crime. But… was the crime really his?

* * *

The two families were neighbours, and their shops stood opposite each other, both equally prosperous, devoid of rivalry or competition. Their black wooden signs displayed red characters, old Vong Cam's reading "Rice Merchant", and that of his friend and partner in long sessions of mah-jong, Tai Sang Leong, "Wine Merchant".

The families often visited each other, and the two men began to exchange confidences. They were worried about the future. There was talk of wars and atrocities committed by the Japanese throughout China, although where they were, life went on normally.

Vong Cam couldn't decide what to do about his son A-Chung's studies, for he was now helping him in his shop and he seemed a thoughtful, hard-working boy. A-Chung was sole inheritor of his father's already considerable fortune, and was destined to take charge of his affairs so as to support his mother and sisters, and the old man's concubines after he died. He resisted the idea of going abroad to further his studies. He had mastered the use of the abacus, he knew a fair number of characters, could read the newspaper, and that was enough.

He felt he would suffer discomfort and inconvenience away from his familiar surroundings. Apart from this, he enjoyed working in his father's business. He knew all about the different qualities of rice, was able to classify them and put the correct price on them; he knew the market, the farmers, and that was all he needed. Even if war broke out in the area, rice was a vital commodity. So his business would certainly not suffer greatly.

Tai Sang Leong didn't have any concubines. His wife had only given him one daughter, and he hadn't sought to force the gods to increase his offspring. Apart from this, his trade in wine was limited in scope. He had begun life by selling the drink from door to door, amid all sorts of difficulties, and so had contented himself with only one wife and the daughter she had given him. Even so, he had three mouths to feed and rice was ever more expensive.

Then, good fortune seemed to protect him, and he set himself up in his little shop, with its red lettering on its sign. Life was good, for his daughter was growing up, brimming with health and beauty, attending schools where she had no difficulty in learning all she was taught.

The young girl was ambitious, and time and time again had hinted at her wish to know the world and experience contact with other folk and other customs. But he wanted her to marry a young man of means, so that she would never go through the hardships that her mother had suffered.

One day, while talking to his old friend Vong Cam, Tai Seng Leong confided his aspirations for his daughter Chan Nui, who was by now fifteen. The two old men, after many exchanges of view, decided their children should marry, and so unite the interests of the two businesses in the future, bringing them both under the one sign.

The two young people obediently agreed with their parents' decision and became engaged, without, however, cultivating their social relations any further. The marriage would take place within three years, with the due pomp that their respective fortunes required.

However, while everything was running serenely in Vong Cam's home, the same was not happening in Tai Sang Leong's, where Chan Nui persisted in pressing her father to allow her to experience something of western civilization before taking on the responsibilities of marriage. She had learned the language of the new world and, through films, admired all she saw of that country, which seemed so attractive to her, with its different lifestyle, habits and customs, and because of the excitement it caused to race through her veins. So insistent was she that her father eventually gave in, but not before getting old Vong Cam's permission. It was decided that Chan Nui would leave for the new world in order to complete her studies, but would not be away for more than two years.

A-Chung didn't mind at all because he had only had the minimum social contact necessary with his fiancée. At home, after his father, he was absolute master, respectfully obeyed by the old man's concubines and by his sisters, with the characteristic submission of Chinese women, who still respect and keep alive the ancient traditions of their country.

For two years, letters and photos from Chan Nui revealed the changes she was undergoing, but the old folk only dwelt on her growing beauty and the marvellous things she told them about that faraway country.

The girl who had left, shy and unsure of herself, came back a perfect woman, elegant, confident in her conversation and firm in her gestures, self-assured and aware of her fine education.

When A-Chung saw her, he realised Chan-Nui would never be like the women of his own household. She was decisive, and spoke to him as an equal, without servility, independent, able to make immediate decisions about how to conduct her life and behave socially.

After a few months, they were married, and Chan Nui's calm air, her purposeful movements and gentle but firm speech stood in flagrant contrast to A-Chung's hesitation and lack of self-confidence.

Beautiful and elegant, she was relaxed as she performed those acts imposed on brides in China, such as kneeling in front of the parents-in-law, traditionally offering them tea, kowtowing submissively before the elder members of both families, and so on.

While A-Chung faltered and floundered, she remained serene and of a natural composure that was enchanting.

For dinner, she set aside the sumptuous dress of scarlet satin embroidered in gold, with its complicated skirts and sashes, and put on an elegant, stylish black satin gown, with a design of leaves in various colours, which gracefully highlighted the seductive contours of her curvaceous body. She was so radiant that gasps of amazement greeted her entrance.

A-Chung, thick set, clumsy and dull next to his slim, fresh, self-confident spouse, was conscious for the first time of his inferiority, but faced with her gracious smile, and the formal deference she was able to show him during the festivities, he banished any unpleasant thoughts.

Chan Nui listened in silence to her husband's opinions and tried to adapt to his manner, but there was something distinguished and impressive about her that nothing could destroy, not even the cut of a less stylish gown, or the absence of lipstick imposed on her by her husband.

In her speech, her walk, her gestures and her attitudes, she was clearly a modern girl, of refined manners, gracious, elegant, and at the same time natural. The two years she had spent in the new world had become imprinted in her delightfully feminine personality.

After five years of marriage, she was the mother of three children, the youngest of whom was only a few months old, born during the period of mourning for A-Chung's father, old Vong Cam, who had departed the world happy for seeing his son in a good marriage, and his business flourishing.

Chan Nui had known how to pay her respects during the

funeral, with all its complex sequence of rituals. In spite of her state, she had not flinched from prostrating herself, touching the ground with her forehead, while weeping for her departed father-in-law. She had put on a white tunic and attended the burial, accompanied by two elderly women servants.

A-Chung could find nothing in his wife except reason for comfort and satisfaction.

Meanwhile, war was spreading and getting nearer. Trade was affected and things started to go badly. Chan Nui's parents and A-Chung's mother met to discuss matters, and it was decided that the young couple would take their three children and leave for the south, so as to protect them from the horrors of war.

So for some months, Shanghai became their refuge. They had taken with them all the money they could muster. The old folk took it upon themselves to send them more later, when they had managed to sell something.

But soon, the Japanese began to bomb Shanghai. The couple and their three little ones fled further south, without being able to get news from home and their family.

Their money began to run low, and they were unable to get any more help from home. In the city where they settled, they knew no one. They moved into a lodging house and waited for hostilities to end. But things got worse, and they had less and less money.

They moved to ever-cheaper lodgings until they ended up in a dark, smoky room behind a guesthouse of dubious repute. There, they slept and ate their rationed bowl of rice, with a few cabbage stalks.

It pained Chan Nui to see her children so ragged and hungry.

Little by little, their best clothes had ended up in the pawnshops. Their cases followed, until all their worldly possessions fitted into two wicker baskets, tied together with string.

A-Chung, downcast, scoured the papers avidly every day, hoping to read that the ever more powerful enemy had been defeated.

China was being consumed by the fire of constant battles, and its people lay crushed, lifeless, in a state of frightful chaos, where all vestige of human solidarity had disappeared.

Chan Nui beseeched her husband to go and find work, but A-Chung had been overcome by apathy and depression, which offered no hope whatsoever of his getting a job. Sometimes, he would set out resolutely from home, only to return at the end of the day, tired and crestfallen, bitter to the point of despair.

No one knew him, and besides, there was hunger all around. Only those prepared to sell themselves to the cruel enemy got any work. All that was left for them to do was to starve to death and watch their children die.

Chan Nui lost her temper. She wasn't prepared to accept such a fate for herself, much less for her children. She berated her husband for the lack of conscience that had got the better of him, for his cowardice, for taking the easy way out. Yes, it was easy to die and let the little ones die, for he wouldn't have to fight, to face up to life, to the difficulties and the horror of their situation. She shouted all her indignation and scorn at him, all of her life's disappointment at being shackled to a creature like him, devoid of any paternal instincts, and she swore she would square up to whatever fate held in store, war, hell, even death itself, in order that her children shouldn't go hungry anymore.

What did she care about prejudice, tradition, decency, dignity, and all those things that made up life's conventional values, if the life they were leading didn't obey any of the rules they were familiar with? If he couldn't get work, she would find the means to provide for her family, if she had to sell her soul or even her body in order to do so.

Shocked by what her words suggested, she collapsed, sobbing convulsively. Her usual air of calm had disappeared completely, and her spirit, hitherto governed by noble concepts, lay like a limp rag between the two of them.

He, pale and with a vacant look in his eye, stared at her in disbelief, while she, distressed and humiliated by her own words, wept bitterly.

Misfortune and tragedy reigned in that painful scene.

Chan Nui dragged herself over to A-Chung, and the two, holding hands, sought to discuss their desperate plight. He cleaned her face and tried to console her. Exhausted, they remained sad and lost in thought. Life was treating them cruelly, but they were young and the war wouldn't last forever. They would face up to their fate, and one day they would be able to tell their children of the pain they were now going through.

Chan Nui would go and look for work in the city's nightclubs, while A-Chung would look after the children. She was young, beautiful, she danced well and there were always people with money, looking for enjoyment. Every night, after putting the children to bed, A-Chung would go and wait for her, and what she earned would enable them to survive the crisis, which couldn't last for much longer.

From the bottom of one of the baskets came the long black satin gown, with its design of coloured leaves, which she had worn at her wedding banquet and had so lovingly kept.

Some relatively peaceful months followed in their home. They no longer had to ration their rice, and there was fish or meat everyday to keep the little ones in noisy happiness. But between the parents, the silence was ever deeper, ever longer. They avoided each other's gaze and more than once, A-Chung threw his chopsticks on the floor in a gesture of revolt against the rice, which had been bought at such a high cost, in return for his dignity as a man and a husband.

It must be said that Chan Nui only danced with the many rich men who sought her there. And, when one day he was tempted to put his arms around her, he saw before him the gown that so many men knew and had in their arms. He felt like tearing it to pieces, but the rice she brought home was vital for their children…

He became taciturn, quick-tempered and nervous, to the point when he would often punish the children. Then, he would come to his senses and weep bitter tears in the privacy of his cubicle, while Chan Nui would spend hours on the dance floor, laughing and in lively conversation.

Her initial reluctance to join such frivolous circles had disappeared, and she became used to a lifestyle, which she now found bearable.

One night, a rich man from a neighbouring city invited her over to his table. The man was of good appearance, well dressed, and spoke the foreign language that she knew so well. They talked for a long time and Chan Nui felt some of her long lost happiness returning. She knew he was a man of wealth, vast wealth, and disposed to spend his money.

At home that night, she unwittingly compared, in her thoughts, that man, so active and full of means, earning pots of money, with her timid, vulgar bumpkin of a husband. She looked at him, full of pity, and closed her eyes so as not to see the harsh reality that she found so distasteful. If her husband were like that, she would never have had to reduce herself to the condition of a nightclub hostess.

She struggled with her conscience all night long, thinking of her children, those three innocent creatures.

A week went by, and then she told A-Chung that she was going to have to accompany someone to a nearby city, for which she hoped to get enough money to be able to give up work once and for all.

Her husband was reluctant, but when she promised to be back within three days, he agreed. Three days would pass quickly, and afterwards, maybe he would be able to set up in business with the money Chan Nui would earn…

She said goodbye to the children, telling them to be good, and promising them sweets and goodies.

A-Chung took her by the arm and repeated insistently: "three days, don't forget, three days."

And so she left quickly, feeling anguished but also happy.

In the neighbouring city, she soon forgot about her wretched existence. She was living a new life, full of light and excitement, with music and glamour that left her starry eyed.

A week went by and she had hardly been aware of time passing. She had been regaled with beautiful things, perfumes and jewellery, sumptuous gowns. She had been infatuated by luxurious and elegant surroundings, she had sat at abundant dinner tables, and tasted the most precious wines, in short, she had lived, lived life to the full…

One morning, lying languidly in her soft bed, she noticed an advertisement. It was A-Chung appealing to her to go home, as their youngest son was dangerously ill. Horrified, Chan Nui forgot everything and caught the first available boat.

When she got home, without any money or presents for the children, she discovered that the advertisement had been a trick by her husband to oblige her to return. She thought of the jewels, of the precious things she had left behind, of the opportunity she had let slip, and she was angry.

Her husband was equally indignant, and likewise screamed his complaints at her, but Chan Nui was mad, stark raving mad.

Forgetting herself completely, she accused him of betraying her, of depriving her of a chance to regain her independence, not just hers, but his and their children's too.

A-Chung, livid with rage, quivering nervously, ran to the sill of the only window in their room, grabbed a kitchen cleaver and submitted Chan Nui to a frenzied attack.

Taken by surprise, she tried to defend herself but it was as if A-Chung were possessed by some hellish, satanic force.

Neighbours rushed forward in answer to her screams, and Chan Nui, lying on the ground, bleeding profusely, with a supreme effort tried to call her children whose voices could be heard as they played in the yard, ignorant of the drama unfolding inside the house.

Hours later, Chan Nui's cruelly mutilated body was carried away in a humble casket.

A-Chung allowed himself to be led away, handcuffed and head hung, his face, body and hands still stained with his victim's blood.

The children were placed in an orphanage by the local authorities, unaware of what had happened.

As he left the room, the wretched man looked around and saw the black satin gown hanging on the back of the door, billowing in the wind, as if provoking him, ironically taunting his suffering soul.

They were unable to squeeze a single tear from him, nor so much as a single word.

And when, some time later, he heard the sentence banishing him to exile in perpetuity, he opened his mouth as if to say something but only a sigh, as if of relief, passed his pale, trembling lips.

Serene, with a serenity he had not known before, he held out his arms to receive the handcuffs, and with firm, decisive step, he followed the guards who led him off to prison.

It was his thirty-second birthday.

AN ACT OF CHARITY

The crowd was heaving, restless and impatient, on the little jetty, eager to complete the duty that social custom required, a duty that was never pleasant when it responded solely to the demands of good manners.

The hour of departure was drawing near and it was time for the young lad to say goodbye, for he was leaving home to continue his studies in a far off land, where he would come to know his father's family.

He scrutinised the crowd, which was becoming ever more packed together because of the narrowness of the quay alongside which the ship was moored. He saw his colleagues, one or two teachers, the few friends his father had, and he frowned at the sight of some people who had been drawn there out of malice and curiosity rather than friendship. As a young man, he felt humiliated by this affront to his pride, which had been hurt ever since he was of tender age, when he had realised how different he was from his companions. This feeling had been the main factor that had impelled him to work assiduously, to spend long hours studying, and to forego his rights as a child, in order to focus only on the marvellous dream of freeing himself from his humiliating predicament.

He felt deeply hurt at the injustice of his life. Why had he been born in those circumstances, if Nature had chosen to endow him with a superior intelligence and consciousness of his sad fate? He asked himself on various occasions whether he would one day escape from the atmosphere of depression that surrounded him, if he would emerge from the shadow cast over him, the humiliating shadow of his illegitimacy. But... he didn't feel guilty, and he suffered from an anger that consumed his whole being. His father, he knew, had come from far, from the ancient continent of Europe, disillusioned by life, embittered and in despair, to hide his pain and maybe his humiliation in that distant part of China. His mother was a poor ignorant Chinese woman, who went around barefoot, had no education whatsoever, and had been brought home one day by the father. There she remained, her situation ill defined, unsure of whether she was just a servant, or a spouse, but without the protection of marriage. But he knew she was his mother, and a mother he loved deep down, while being ashamed of her in society, a mother he didn't like to be seen with, and who didn't understand him. She was the mother who had given birth to him, raised him and fed him, but who smacked him during moments of uncontained anger, and whose lack of education led her to shout at him, heaping all her accusations and frustration upon him when, in his childish mischief, he got in her way.

His father rarely engaged him in conversation, for he understood little of his language, but he himself had learned to speak both languages without difficulty, so that he could understand both his parents. He had never seen them go out together, they never went for a walk in each other's company, never exchanged ideas about their life together. Ever since he had reached the age of awareness, he had noticed that his father gave the orders and his mother merely obeyed them submissively. At table, she ate her bowl of rice with chopsticks, while he and his father had knives, forks and spoons. Christmas festivities and other such occasions were not observed in their house. When he was ill, his father took him to a European doctor, but his mother would in turn call a medicine man. Then, there were the arguments and the vexation. He found himself obliged to calm his father's rage and explain to his mother why his father was so insistent on the need for a doctor. He listened bewildered to the complaints of both sides and felt secretly miserable.

Why had he been born like that? Why? Why?

He hugged his friends, dry eyed, thanking them for their good wishes, but as he held out his hand to those he knew were not there out of friendship, he felt a type of dizziness, but then controlled himself, for he would soon be free of all those things he found repugnant.

His father opened his arms to him and he allowed himself to be clasped in an embrace he was unable to return. He hated himself at that moment, but he couldn't be blamed for what he was feeling in his heart. This man was his father, a father who, in his homespun rudeness, would heap his affection upon him, a father who, in his gruff language, always privileged him with an all-consuming love, as if to make up for his sad life.

He wished he could feel proud of this man who had tried to protect him from all manner of adversity during his life, but all he could feel was pity. It was, after all, him he had to thank for the life he hated, he was the one responsible for it.

He felt a desire, a burning desire for affection, a consuming desire to be able to hold both father and mother in the same embrace, but they were not the parents he would have chosen for himself, they could not satisfy his childhood ambitions, so often felt when he was small, when he had asked himself why he didn't have parents like other children. Now he knew that he would soon be free of this situation, soon he would be able to frequent a new circle of friends and companions, without having to put up with the curious looks of those who seemed to seek in his physiognomy some confirmation of the stigma of his origins.

He had worked, studied, shut his ears to the cruel gossip, and was now leaving to conquer for himself the name he lacked, the self-esteem of which he had always been deprived, so as to feel unencumbered and the equal of others.

He had asked his mother not to go with him to the quayside, but had taken his leave of her with a sore heart, for he knew he would never see her again, but he had been embarrassed by the extravagance of her gestures, the cries she had let out, the absurd demonstration of sadness at their parting, that were so typical of her. He watched her dry her eyes on the sleeve of her gown, witnessed once again her primitive, clumsy behaviour, and fled, half sad, half relieved.

Absent mindedly, he shook the hands held out to him. Nearby, a fellow traveller reminded him to hurry, as the ship was about to leave.

Then suddenly, he stopped short, as if struck. Nearby, a Chinese woman, sobbing profusely, was trying to push towards him through the crowd. Her unkempt appearance, and the way in which she expressed her sorrow in loud wailing, revealed her social class, the working woman she was, even though her face didn't suggest any such hardship in recent years.

The young man's face took on a severe expression, which was accentuated by his pallor, and his eyes sought out his father. He, however, quickly moved away, as if unable to face up to such a scene.

When the woman managed to get near him, and before she

could give vent to her sorrows, he felt in his waistcoat pocket, and pulling out a coin, dropped it in her hands, which were outstretched before his eyes as if in prayer. Then, trembling nervously, he moved quickly away, and strode feverishly up the gangplank and onto the ship.

Down on the quay, with bewildered look, and wailing loudly, the woman kept repeating as she was racked by sobs:

"He gave me his charity, he gave me a dime, in return for the life I gave him!"

A CONFLICT OF FEELINGS

On the quayside, a compact, heaving mass of people jostled together in that matter-of-fact way, which is characteristic of large crowds. The buzz was deafening. Some were leaving, others had just come to watch the great ship leave for the New World, that distant America, land of promise for so many who had suffered painful times and the harshest privations in their poverty stricken land of China.

Sitting on a suitcase, one could see a woman of little more than forty years of age, thin and wizened, her rough hands revealing a lifetime of hard work, her face pallid. Only her eyes seemed feverish, as if within that almost skeletal body, there was a soul struggling to overcome pain and disappointment. Nearby, her son, a young lad of ten, his eyes deep and dark like his mother's, his face full and smiling, was saying goodbye to his family with an air of indifference, as if there mingled within him an intense wish to begin the journey that would take him faraway, to that fabulous country he had learned about through letters from his maternal uncle, the man who was now summoning him.

The mother watched her son's gestures with a melancholy air, paying particular attention to the father, whose sixty years weighed upon him more like eighty. Nearby, her husband's other wives chatted away happily. This was the husband she was now leaving, in order to help her son find a life in America, after he had received such praise from teachers and friends on account of his rare intelligence.

Her cold, apathetic look, made an impression on her husband, who, down the years, had become used to seeing in her someone who lacked any will of her own, a disillusioned soul who accepted impassively her share of life's joys and pains.

As her dark eyes surveyed the distance, she seemed to be reliving the past fifteen years, ever since she had returned to China, where her son had been born after five years of marriage. She recalled the fun loving girl she had once been, the happiness she had felt at being chosen for a wife by that rich merchant, whose first wife had died some time before.

Born and brought up in America, she had attended schools where the traditions of her country were often the subject of discussion, where she had learned to have such a different view of life that when she arrived in Mother China, she openly criticised the custom of allowing men to have more than one wife.

Her husband introduced her to his friends with barely concealed pride. He had taken a well-educated, cultured wife, who was his equal, and in many ways superior to him. She took such an active part in his business ventures that these began to prosper by leaps and bounds.

But gradually he surrendered to the constant invitations from his friends and began to frequent meetings from which women were barred. He gambled almost every day, dined noisily, and drank himself silly.

When he arrived home, he listened ashamedly to the complaints of his wife, who one day gave him the good news that she was going to have a child.

He could hardly contain himself with joy. When the baby was born, it was a healthy boy.

When the child was one month old, he threw a party, as was the custom, spending lavishly, and inviting friends and mere acquaintances to a sumptuous banquet.

For a while, he stopped meeting his friends, but little by little, he began once again to frequent clubs and theatres, and to gamble heavily.

One day, he announced to his wife that he had decided to take a concubine, given that she could hardly accompany him in his social life, busy as she always was with their son. She made a terrible scene, and reminded him of what he had promised, her principles, as well as the commitment she had undertaken. He invoked his rights as a Chinese husband, reminding her that they were not in America.

From that day onwards, she underwent a deep change in her appearance. No one saw her laugh anymore, no one heard her utter a word unless it was necessary. She was polite to her husband and the other woman, who now sat at table with an impertinent air, got up late and treated her with scorn.

But a year had hardly gone by before another woman joined them at table. This one was still younger and slim. Her pale face caused her make-up to stand out like an insolent flash of colour.

She was now devoid of further feelings. Her indifference increased with time. Their standard of living began to decline, for her husband neglected his business interests, until one day, he declared himself bankrupt. At the time, he had four concubines.

It was then that her brother came up with the idea of sponsoring her son to go to America, by paying his passage. Her husband gave his consent immediately, for the boy was intelligent and good at his studies. Apart from this, he would rid himself of his greatest responsibility. When she went to tell him that she was going with her son, her husband shouted in her face, claiming he didn't have the money for her fare. She didn't answer, but merely showed him her rough hands, her wrinkled face, her greying hair and her thin, wizened body. Then, she set about packing her few gowns, which she herself had made out of cheap cloth.

She was taking her son away in order that he should be spared a fate such as hers, full of toil and uncertainty, but as the days passed, her spirit was weighed down by a terrible misgiving. She kept asking herself whether she had the right to abandon the old man, who would be left in the hands of his ever more demanding and extravagant concubines. But then her thoughts would turn to her son, and her responsibility towards his education.

On the day of their departure, she heard her husband complaining that he didn't feel well. Immediately, she felt her breast tighten. Then, they all went down to the quay, and the inner conflict that had arisen at this decisive moment in her life opened a fresh wound in her heart. Her son's indifference shocked her. She wanted him to show respect and affection, but the child's airs seemed to reveal a strong will and energetic temperament.

She glanced at her husband and saw that he was downcast and feeble. She felt remorse for the decision she had taken. And what if she were to tell him she had decided not to go? There was still time. Her son would go to his uncle's house and be well treated there. He was young, whereas her husband couldn't have long to live. She got up, and with her heart beating fast, she walked towards him, hesitantly, almost ashamed.

At that very moment, she suddenly felt someone push past. In front of her, she saw an elegant young woman, fresh and smiling, whom her husband seemed to be devouring with his gaze. Then, in an attempt to attract the girl's attention, he followed and tried to engage her in conversation.

Her whole life, along with her husband's true personality, revealed themselves to her there and then. He would never change. He had squandered his fortune but what he had left was used up on his expensive conquests.

She raised her head, as if shaking a strange weight from her. Her lips opened in a confident smile. She had been on the point of opening herself up to new hardships and disappointment. She had almost thrown away the chance to educate her son according to her standards, merely in order to protect her sick and elderly husband from the frivolity of his concubines.

How had she allowed herself to be deceived by such a display of feigned decrepitude?

Taking her son by the hand, she walked swiftly up the gangplank. Her life, her new life began to open out in front of her on the far horizon, upon which the Sun cast its light, full of promise.

THE SUFFERING OF LIN FONG

Evening was falling serenely over Ou Mun, and that gentle light that precedes the appearance of the stars in the blue sky, surrounding the purple of eastern sunsets, left Lin Fong with an acute but inexplicable sense of sadness. It sapped her fingers of the usual nimbleness with which she would roll the firecrackers on her little wooden wheel.

Amidst the din made by the women in the huge factory, her silence spoke far louder than the voices that filled the large building, with its four whitewashed walls and its ceiling, where the beams that supported the roof had long turned black.

The siren signalled the end of the shift, and Lin Fong went and handed in her basket, which was always full. She held out her pale, trembling hand to receive her day's wages, and shuddered at the sight of such a pittance. Shut away there hour after hour, bent over her wheel, suffering heat and cold, the base of her spine in agony at having to sit in such an uncomfortable position, all for a wage that didn't even amount to one *pataca*. What would her mother say? She who was riddled with tuberculosis, and who watched her arrive every day, to see whether she had enough money to make her some soup, just as the doctor had prescribed.

Rice took up most of their daily amount of money, and mother and daughter contented themselves with a few vegetable stalks, or one or two little salt fish as an accompaniment.

But no matter how much she tried, she couldn't do as much work as she had in the old days, when she was considered the best worker in the factory. Of course, that was the only reason they kept her on, for A-Cheoc, the supervisor who had lusted after her for so long, didn't have spirit enough to understand the needs of her sick mother, or her own sorrows.

She left, her head bowed in thought as she prepared another excuse for her mother, who did not spare her from complaints and accusations. She set off along the road home, but just as she had for the past few months, she paused in front of the temple, unsure of whether she should go in or not. The goddess Cun Iam seemed to have forgotten her, and no matter how many times she knelt before her, touching the floor with her forehead, the goddess remained impassive towards her intense suffering. No, on that day she wouldn't go in, for she wanted to believe life had some happiness in store for her when "he" returned from Sai Iong, where he had been sent so suddenly.

She recalled those calm, peaceful evenings when she would stroll along the waterfront by his side, watching the junks as they sailed elegantly into the harbour. She remembered how he spoke, and how strange it had seemed at first until she got used to guessing what he meant, the way he squeezed her hand hard, the times she had had to avoid his embraces and kisses, things she was unfamiliar with. She recalled A-Cheoc's suspicious look when she had told him that she would not marry as long as her mother was alive, and his look of silent, angry disgust when he saw her one evening sitting by the water next to "him".

The following day, as she left work, he chastised her, laid into her shame with obscene insults, accusing his rival of dishonest intentions. Was she naïve enough to believe the European would marry her, an illiterate factory worker, whose only attraction was the freshness of her youth and the promise of a gracious body under her cotton gown?!

Lin Fong felt deeply hurt and decided to prove that "he" was different from the rest, because "he" talked to her about his country, his mother, and promised that one day he would show her the fields full of wheat and the snow capped mountains.

She felt a surge of blood through her veins every time "he" lovingly put his arm round her waist, while the thought of A-Cheoc, with his absurd insinuations, filled her with anger.

It was true that "he" had never spoken to her of marriage, but his promise to take her with him all the way to Sai Iong must surely be tantamount to a matrimonial intent. She satisfied herself that he was probably acting in accordance with "his" customs. Later, she only felt happy when she was by his side, and all but lived for the moment when he would come to her, as the sun set, always eager for her attentions and caresses. She was gripped by madness and she completely forgot A-Cheoc and his warnings. He was totally worthy of her trust, all her love, and even her complete surrender. She felt proud to see him happy, to know that "he" owed all his joy to her, that it was she who kept him forever smiling.

Weeks went by and then, one night, she had to tell him her secret, which wasn't just hers, but theirs, the secret that would make "him" intensely happy when he found out. "He" had shown concern, even irritation and anger at her circumstances. But in the end, he calmed her fears and told her everything would be resolved.

At the factory, A-Cheoc kept glancing at her surreptitiously, noticed how pale she was, how tired her eyes looked, noticed her indisposition, which caused her to get up from her work so often. He even asked her whether her discomfort was all due to the charms of her foreign devil lover.

She remained quiet, without the strength to answer him. Humiliated, she listened to his ironic laughter, and even wished she were like the other girls, and had never left the tight circle of poverty for the moments of pleasure "he" had shown her. So much happiness surely exacted its price, and the pain she now felt was surely life's payment.

One evening, "he" came to tell her he was leaving unexpectedly, that he was required to return along with the other soldiers to his distant country, but he promised to come back to fetch her. As for their secret, she would surely know how to get by without his help.

Lin Fong didn't even shed a tear. The horror of her predicament had devastated her. She went home in a daze. The next morning, she missed work in order to go and see the soldiers off. Hiding behind a tree, she managed to make him out, his haversack on his back. He seemed smaller now, as she watched him among his boisterous, happy companions. "He" looked slightly sad, and she felt some consolation for that. She emerged from her hiding place, and walked over to where she could be seen. "He" saw her and nodded. It was enough for her to feel less unhappy, less distraught. Then, once aboard, he waved to her with a coloured handkerchief she had once given him. At that moment, she felt elated, and the secret life inside her made its presence felt with a sudden violent shudder.

Ever since that day, Lin Fong has lived through her torment, waiting for him to return from Sai Iong to hear the first cry of the child she had given him, in exchange for a few fleeting moments of happiness, for the intense pain of uncertainty, for the fear of being found out, and the consequences she was bound to suffer.

THE JADE RING

She had been fascinated by the sight of jade ever since she was very young. She was awestruck every time she looked at the bright green of its cold, smooth surface. Nature had made her fragile, her skin pellucid, her eyes almond shaped, dark and always shining, her hair black and abundant, and tied in plaits, in the traditional Chinese manner.

Her voice had a seductive ring, full of some vague sadness as if she had guessed ever since the cradle what fate had in store for her.

When she was still little, scarcely eight years old, she was taken to a rich household where she was to be the companion and servant to a girl of her age, spoilt and impertinent, who took pleasure in tugging her plaits until it hurt. She hardly cared that she was given the leftovers from the dining table to eat, that she had to sleep on a mat on the floor of the young girl's bedroom, and that she got woken up merely out of spite, every time her mistress knew she was particularly tired or sleepy. In summer, she would stand by the nice soft bed and fan her mistress who would bite her whenever she felt like it.

She would stare, fascinated, at an oval shaped jade ring encircled by diamonds that the lady of the house wore, and she would forget all her duties.

Whenever she came across the ring lying around somewhere, she would stand there contemplating it with devotion, without daring to even touch it.

And so life proceeded without any great changes. She grew slowly, but was always slim, while the girl she served was ever more plump. She had learnt to read and write merely because she had attended the other girl's lessons, but her education had stopped right there when she was obliged to wait outside the school for rich kids that her young mistress went to later on. But she amused herself by reading whatever she could get hold of.

And the years went by…

That day was her seventeenth birthday, a secret she kept closely to herself. No one had ever bothered to find out when her birthday was, and she had never been given a present, nor ever received any good wishes. But that year, things were going to be different.

She would recall, enraptured, the looks she had received from a gentleman in a long gown, with slender aristocratic hands who, one day, as she paused from her tasks, had shown her the beautiful pictures he himself had painted. Afterwards, he had asked her name, how she had come to be there, what her situation was in that house. In short, here was someone who showed an interest in her life and the course it was taking.

She took her leave and left the house one evening in order to start a new life, guided by those aristocratic hands that handled a paintbrush with such skill.

They set up home in a small, elegant house, surrounded by a

high wall, with large windows and comfortable furniture. An elderly maid was awaiting their arrival and praised her freshness and fine figure the moment she came into the house with her master. And she felt happy, happier than she could ever have dreamt.

She spent her days leafing through books and magazines, carefully combing her hair and learning the graceful manners she had admired in the women she had served for so many years. She ate with ivory chopsticks from a bowl of fine porcelain. She did a little sewing and was dazzled by all the clothes she could now call her own.

And so her life slipped smoothly by in that gilded cage, for rarely was she allowed to leave the house. Occasionally she would go to the Chinese opera with the old maid, and sometimes she would go out at night with the man who had come into her life like a true god, and who often had to leave her on her own because of some business commitment or other. But she was happy, especially when he came back with a present that thrilled her.

Five years went by…

One day, she opened the newspaper and saw a photo of her master next to a richly dressed lady, whom she recognized as her former mistress. At first she didn't attach any importance to it, for she belonged to a different class, but when she realized that it was a forthcoming wedding announcement, she collapsed on the floor. The maid rushed to her aid, but she could barely take in the old woman's words as she attempted to explain the complexities of her situation. She cried for the whole day and was unable to eat anything.

At night she cleaned her face and tried to behave as serenely as possible, for she hoped that the news was not true, and that he would hasten to explain things to her.

When the bell rang, she put on a smile, but couldn't hide her state of mind.

He came in as usual, in a joyous mood, wanting to know how she had spent the day. Then, from an inside pocket he took out a little round metal box, painted red. She opened it hurriedly and took out a beautiful jade ring, surrounded by gems. She put it on her finger and was ecstatic. A jade ring such as she had always wanted and was now hers!

Suddenly, she remembered and showed him the newspaper. He shrugged his shoulders and explained that their life wouldn't change in any way.

But she wouldn't listen to him. She threw the ring that had been her gilded dream at his feet and fled. He tried to run after her but then decided to stay where he was… and he picked up the precious ring. She was bound to come back once she had got over her emotional outburst.

* * *

Two days later, the sea washed up a disfigured body. Only the abundant hair seemed to proclaim its identity. No one claimed the mortal remains, and early one morning, a rough coffin was being taken to the cemetery, when a well-dressed man, with slender, aristocratic hands, joined the procession. At the graveside, he gave the pallbearers a generous tip to stand aside and uncovering the body, he placed a beautiful ring encircled with gems on one of the fingers.

Then he hurried off.

Some time later, the newspapers announced the wedding of a

famous painter and the daughter of an important businessman, which had been attended by the cream of society.

THE MODEL

Ever since she was a child, Daphne had been graced with an astounding beauty. This was to be the instrument of her later happiness and subsequent tragedy.

She was born in Shanghai, of a Chinese mother and American father, and Nature had been extremely generous with its endowments. She had a clear, delicate skin, silky black hair, a graceful mouth, and violet eyes fringed abundantly with long, dark eyelashes that gave her clear calm look a mysterious appeal.

By the time she was seventeen, she was a beauty who filled her parents with pride. She spoke various languages and captivated people with her innocent, modest air. Her father dreamt of a brilliant future for her, and had taken great care over her education.

The war in China had deprived him of a considerable fortune, but he was still young, and decided to go and rebuild his assets in America.

His daughter, Daphne, was going to get to know a different

world and might gain a better future than in China.

For two years, the family lived happily until, one morning, Daphne's father died unexpectedly. A car accident had changed her life.

Daphne suffered the shock as any youngster would who had lost the firm support of a father, experienced in life's struggles. Her mother allowed herself to be completely overcome with grief.

The girl had to confront problems she had never dreamt she would have to face. It was up to her now to earn a living for herself and her mother. Friends helped her to get a job in an advertising agency. Her beauty made her a favourite for modelling assignments among photographers and designers.

Soon she was known as the most sought after model. Everything looked good on her, from the most exotic hat to the strangest pair of sandals. Jewellery, a dress, a flower all looked prettier when she was wearing them.

Her perfect oval face with its mixture of European and Asian features appeared everywhere, and she had many admirers.

When people talked about her, they just referred to *The Model*. Daphne had disappeared to be replaced by *The Model*.

She surrounded her mother with comforts. She installed her in an elegant room, with enough servants to satisfy her every whim. Her daughter was always busy and could hardly devote any time to her. But on Sundays, she would take her for trips into the countryside or to the nearby towns.

The Model was the focus of attention wherever she went. Her natural beauty was an ideal basis for the elegant and stunning personality into which she had been transformed.

It was she who displayed all the latest whims of fashion. She dressed at the expense of the most famous fashion houses, all of which competed for her favours. She would regularly receive the most expensive perfumes, as well as a multitude of creams, powders and lipsticks. Her name was a guarantee of success for any manufacturer of cosmetics.

At the same time, her fortune was growing. She was barely twenty-two, and her financial assets were the envy of many.

Life smiled at her, and Daphne was in no hurry to change direction. She could get married and abandon her career, but she found the high life attractive. What was more, she enjoyed the company of young people of her own age, whether they were designers or models. *The Model* was loved by all and knew how to please everyone, without distinction.

One day, dressed in a few dozen yards of fine white silk, with her black hair loose over her shoulders, she was posing languidly when suddenly, her dress caught fire after brushing against someone's cigarette. Before anyone could free her, she was engulfed in flames that spread rapidly through the studio.

She was horribly burnt. After two months in hospital, she returned home. In spite of the numerous operations she had undergone, she was a shadow of her former beautiful self.

Her mother took the shock badly. With an already weak heart, she died soon afterwards.

This time, Daphne faced her tragedy with strength. By now she was even richer, for she had received a huge sum in damages. She looked around her and reached a decision. She had had some wonderful times. The future shouldn't be sad. She directed her energies to adopting young orphan girls, and turned her house into an art school. There she encouraged her unfortunate girls to concentrate on rebuilding their lives, giving them an education and preparing them to face up to the great crises of life with courage.

Her decision won the admiration of all those who knew her. She uttered not a single word of resentment or anger. Once again she was Daphne, but to those who knew her story, she would always be *The Model*, except that now she was a model far more worthy of being copied.

HENRIQUE DE SENNA FERNANDES

Born in Macau in 1923, he graduated in law in 1952 from Coimbra University, Portugal, where he wrote his first fiction. He worked as a teacher in a number of educational institutions in Macau, as well as running his own law office, which he established upon returning to his native city. He has written widely for the press, and is the author of two collections of short stories, *Nam Van* (1978) and *Mong Há* (1998), as well as two novels, *Amor e Dedinhos de Pé* (1986) and *A Trança Feiticeira* (1993), both of which were turned into films.

TEA WITH ESSENCE OF CHERRY

Every time I turn the corner of the old Rua da Alfândega and walk down the Rua da Felicidade, I hear my friend Maurício's hearty peal of laughter, which sprang straight from his heart. I see his huge frame outlined against the buildings and I recall with longing his company, his spontaneous joy and his all embracing presence.

I can't remember when I first met him. I only recall that we became friends when we were both in the third grade at primary school, at the time when it was located near the beginning of the Calçada da Gamboa.

What times those were! We had a very efficient teacher, although she was very bad tempered and shouted for no reason at all. May God rest her soul but I only ever remember her being angry and screaming at us.

She spared us neither stinging whacks with the ruler nor blows that left bumps on our head.

At that time I was a skinny little kid who wore smart clothes.

Maurício, on the other hand, was a poor boy, badly dressed, who would arrive at school racked with cold when the northerly winds were blowing from China.

He was about four years older than I was, and the son of a Portuguese father and a *bambina*, which in the dialect of Macau, means a foundling or orphan, taken in and raised by the nuns. In spite of his difficult childhood, he had grown up without any discernible rancour or envy. Living in different circles, we apparently had little in common.

But the truth was that we became friends.

Maurício belonged to the group of truants, and the teacher put him at the back of the huge classroom, in the part the children called the chicken house. It was the area for the idlers, those repeating the year for the first or second time, and as in those days there was no upper age limit, it was the tough guys' den. There was one who had turned eighteen, although Maurício himself was no more than thirteen.

While we, the youngsters, inhabited the front rows, under constant terror of the irritable schoolmistress, those at the back amused themselves at the expense of the poor lady. Blows with the ruler, boxing of the ears, raps over the head had not the slightest effect. Nor even did the punishment where you had to kneel in the corner of the room, your face turned towards the wall, and you were deprived of the only half-hour break of the day from ten thirty to eleven. Maurício would tell me in his trumpeting voice:

"I've got a thick skin."

The teacher insisted on complete silence, as if that were possible in a place brimming with kids yearning to get out into the street and the sunshine. Those at the back expressed their resentment of the harsh atmosphere, making their ancient desks creak, coughing loudly, or getting up at every opportunity to ask to go to the "little room". They took it in turns, putting on the most desperate expressions, almost always in the middle of an important grammar lesson, which we all feared.

It was an exhausting struggle for the unfortunate lady. Not infrequently, she became so nervous that she would pick up a closed inkpot and hurl it in the direction of the pupil who was taxing her patience. At the first sign of this action, someone would shout:

"Grenade!"

We would all, as of one, hide our heads in our arms, flat out against our desks, while the projectile passed over us. This was one of the educational techniques used in my youth!

In spite of everything, I am grateful to that teacher, whose draconian methods I shall never forget, for having taught me to conjugate verbs, especially the irregular ones. What I can't forget either is that she forced us, for it featured in our geography textbook, to learn by heart all the railway stations in every single branch line in Continental Portugal, as well as all the tributaries of the main rivers, in addition to the mountain ranges. One day, when Mogoflores station escaped me, I got my ears pulled, a harsh punishment that I considered most unfair, and indeed still do, for at the time I had only ever seen a train in the cinema, and couldn't even imagine what a railway station was, much less the one at Mogoflores. I can still feel the pain of that tugging at my ears to this day.

I don't know why – and today I understand it even less – I wasn't liked by some of the bigger boys. They pushed the younger ones around, but no one interfered with me once Maurício declared himself my protector. And this started when a certain big bully got at me one day because I wouldn't give him some food I had with me. He was so insulting that I answered back in kind. That was enough for him to challenge me to a trial of strength at half past three that afternoon, after school. The place where these fights traditionally took place was next to the leafy pagoda tree, which still stands, in front of the Sir Robert Ho Tung Library, not far from the rear entrance to the St Joseph Seminary.

I was frozen with fear, but with all the bravado of a knight of Calatrava, I accepted the challenge. How I suffered waiting for the fatal hour when school finished! But in the end, nothing happened to me. Maurício accompanied me to the shade of the tree and shouted at the great hulk that he should be ashamed of himself for having challenged a little kid to an unequal fight. He took on the role of my defender, and hurled such abuse at the other that he had no choice but to accept him as my substitute. They immediately started to grapple with each other, trading heavy punches, and if it hadn't been for some very unevangelical blows with an umbrella from a passing priest, interrupted in his reading of the breviary, there would have been many more stinging punches exchanged. It doesn't matter who came off worse. What was certain is that no one ever again interfered with me. I remained eternally grateful to Maurício.

I also recall that I very rarely bought exercise books and other school material during that year. It wasn't that my parents were mean in such matters, on the contrary, they were positively generous. But Maurício inculcated in me the idea that I should save my money for more useful things, assuring me that he would provide me with whatever I needed. After school, he would go to the Po Man Lau Bookshop and to the Rua dos Mercadores, where there were many stationery shops in those days. The following day, he would bring me exercise books, nibs, rubbers, pencils and pens, pilfered with a cunning that would make you shiver. My parents' allowance was used to buy Chinese sweets, succulent pieces of sugar cane and corn on the cob, which were sold outside the school door. I have especially tender memories of that year when I enjoyed, almost exclusively, Maurício's warm friendship. I envied his self-confidence, the way he walked down the street as if it belonged to him.

We passed the third grade exam. However, he, who was no fool but just plain lazy, got a ten out of twenty.

"That's the hardest average to reach."

What mattered was to pass.

It was because of his struggle to get through the year and obtain such a mark, that I was always sympathetic to tens. Moreover, as I ended up with many a ten in my studies, I always held the mark in high esteem.

Maurício and I had a great time together over the holidays, as if nothing could separate us. We would go to the bathing huts at Tai-Pan Beach, along the Outer Harbour. We would fly our kites, making them dip and cut in front of those of our adversaries. On long afternoons, we would explore the abundant pine wood on Guia hill, building hidey holes and living like Tarzan. It's not easy to erase from one's memory a happy-go-lucky, untroubled time, when nothing in the world could tarnish our joy and our thirst for life.

We went through fourth grade like this too. Once we had completed our primary school, I went on to the Lycée, and he to the Commercial School. We thus ceased being inseparable. He started to have new friends, naturally enough seeking out people of his own age and from the same school. But our friendship continued over the years. Every now and then, we would go for long walks, as if we were trying, in a few hours, to make up for all the time we spent each in our own circle.

On those occasions, he would explain himself, telling me all about his life, his many adventures, his day-to-day existence. Here and there, he would stop when he saw some girls, directing flirtatious comments to them that would never have occurred to me, and which seemed all the more facile once uttered. With his fluent Chinese, he was the terror of the Cheok-Chai-Un quarter, where he wooed the maids with their thick braids and the girls who went to the fountain to fill their buckets with drinking water.

When I told him I dreamt of continuing my studies in Portugal, he didn't envy me. He merely said that I had been born a luckier man than he had. He never talked about his family, and he avoided any reference to his home life, which I knew was beset by problems of money. But he never showed any shame. He just liked life on the streets more than he did his parents' home.

He never finished his commercial course or anything like it. He went through some extravagant failures while there, and fell behind, while I was cruising through the Lycée. One evening, he turned up on my doorstep to say goodbye. He was going to Hong Kong to become a pilot, a foible that led many Macau lads to emigrate at the time. His parents died, one after the other, during his absence.

Months later, the War of the Pacific broke out, with all its tragic results. My dreams of continuing my studies were for the moment destroyed. War, which encircled Macau and afflicted it with famine, put an end to any chance of my plans being fulfilled. I would have to wait for peace, which was still a long way off.

In those troubled circumstances, which of course brought the entire city to its knees, I forgot all about Maurício. Apart from anything else, I was concerned with my own survival and that of my family, and had little time to worry about anything else. All I knew was that he had returned to Macau, among the various levies of refugees who arrived every day from Hong Kong and other parts of China occupied by the Japanese. Then, during the first year of the war, our paths crossed on a number of occasions, but we had neither the time nor the patience to talk, malnourished and distressed as we were.

I can remember one particularly painful winter's morning as I stood in the bread queue, amongst people with squalid, haggard faces. I caught sight of Maurício, trembling with cold, the collar of his cape drawn up, barely protecting him from the north wind. His nose was a deep red and dripping with snot. He was three people ahead of me. He waved and, for the first time, I caught him downcast, defeated by adversity. This time, he seemed ashamed to see me. He smiled feebly and then hunched his shoulders in an anguished display of dejection.

I have no idea how Maurício got by during that terrible year. Having finished the seventh grade, I got a job for we had to earn our daily crust and there was never enough money to satisfy the black market that cropped up all over the city, despite measures taken to stamp it out. I still caught the occasional glimpse of him, he was always in a hurry, terribly thin, with his meagre body swimming in his suit.

But Maurício was one of life's survivors. It wasn't in his temperament to give up, passive and resigned, and wait for death, like someone offering his neck to the executioner's knife. He had the spirit of a fighter. He threw himself into jobs that paid badly, and stuck to nothing. It was as if he were riddled with woodworm, as the old ladies of Macau used to say.

After the first year of war, which was the worst one, I noticed he was dressing better. He would even pause to talk to me in the street. He promised to arrange to meet me for longer, but he never had time. He was frequenting dubious circles, people on the make, an altogether frightening example of fauna that the times threw up, greedily joining speculative enterprises, and taking advantage of the extraordinary openings that circumstances offered. At first, people were taken aback, but then they got used to the tragedies and difficulties of everyday life. They became hardened and began to accept as natural the horrendous things happening before their eyes.

"It's war…" people commented and excused everything.

The conflict provided its own unique opportunities for shady dealings, which filled the pockets of the lucky and the quick witted, those with few scruples and enough audacity. New rich appeared like mushrooms, living in the most ostentatious luxury. Both extremes lived side by side, the most abject poverty on the one hand, and the most offensive wealth on the other.

With the second year of the war well underway, Maurício came looking for me more frequently. He would telephone me at the office, and we would arrange to meet, out of preference, at the Delícias bar of the Hotel Riviera, so as to hear Art Carneiro's orchestra playing at the tea dances. He would now turn up with a wallet bulging with five-hundred *pataca* notes, while mine contained a few grubby fifty cent ones. Times had certainly changed for Maurício! He displayed amazing generosity, and wouldn't allow me to plunder my meagre wages.

"My money comes and goes. Yours is fixed and is never more than that pittance. Besides, my day had to come."

He openly scorned marriage. He made a deliberate show of his links with prostitutes. With a knowing air, he declared that women only served one function. Of course, such a thing could only come from the mouth of someone who had never truly had a home life.

I never asked him where his money came from. This was a taboo subject during the war. But I advised him to establish himself on a firmer basis, and to think about the future.

His reply came back at me like a whiplash:

> "You're right, in part. But who could earn what I earn? I'm going to come out of this war loaded. It's my only chance. Either I end up rich or I die. For me, there's no choice."

I guessed how, deep down, he had hated being poor, despised, suffering privations.

Now, he flaunted his wealth as an act of defiance, in a wish to tell everyone in no uncertain terms that he was opulent and didn't need condescension or pity from anyone. He was a self-made man and he was proud of it.

I'm not going to recount all I know about the fascinating figure of Maurício. It is not my intention to write his biography nor even to relate his numerous adventures, which could fill a book.

I shall limit myself to telling an episode involving my friend in the Rua da Felicidade, which would have unforeseen consequences for him.

Whoever walks down the Rua da Felicidade nowadays, won't find anything unusual about it. It is now a partly residential, partly commercial street, packed with eating houses and little else. But those who evoke its past, will be aware that it was the heart of Macau's love quarter, forming part of the old Bazar, whose remains lost all their original character when new avenues were drawn through it and the Chinese residents, at least on the surface, radically altered their lifestyles.

The Bazar was the quintessential Chinese city of Macau. Its

labyrinth of lanes, alleyways and streets seethed with a noisy, bustling population, occupied in a thousand and one activities. This made it very different from the areas inhabited predominantly by the Portuguese, and which, in bygone days, made up the so-called Christian City, a quiet, sleepy provincial town. To one side of a line running through the areas of Lilau, S. Lourenço, Santo Agostinho, Largo do Senado, Monte and Santo António, the Chinese City began, fanning out along the Inner Harbour. All manner of trade was conducted there, and a huge multitude of people jostled and worked from sun up to sun down, in stinking, unhygienic little streets that greatly dismayed anyone coming to the City of the Name of God for the first time, and who came ashore from the river.

Its population was not only composed of natives of Macau. There were folk from various parts of the Chinese territory adjacent to the city, who went there for business or pleasure. Macau served all Heong San, for which it was also the natural outlet, and the Inner Harbour monopolized the transit trade with its rich hinterland. Nor should we forget that there was a sizeable floating and fishing population, anchored in the river, which came ashore in its free time.

The Bazar had everything. Boarding houses and inns, goldsmiths and money changers, eating houses, the so-called *fantims* and *cou-laus*, small-time tailors and pawnshops, junk shops and a whole variety of other enterprises, an entire alleyway full of scrap metal dealers, a whole street selling silk and other cloth. At the very heart of this city, the *fantan* houses with their typical façades, stood out, along with lottery shops, smoking dens, *flower houses* and other brothels of lesser category.

Transport was mainly by rickshaw, carts pulled by human traction, which gradually took the place of sedan chairs. The thoroughfares were packed with street sellers uttering their time-honoured cries. Another typical sight were the scrap metal men, the famous *tin-tins* who invaded the streets, beating a metal plate with a little piece of iron and producing the sound that gave them their name.

Now, cutting through from the top of the Rua da Alfândega as far as the old Fat Siu Lau restaurant, and extending on as far as the Rua Cinco de Outubro, was the Rua da Felicidade, with its authentic grey brick Chinese houses, which had high doors, and along the top of their façade a carved frieze recounting scenes from ancient Chinese legends, with inscriptions no doubt alluding to the nature of the street's business. This was the centre of the love quarter, which spread out into surrounding alleys and side streets, and which, together, was dedicated to one sole purpose: pleasure.

By day, the Rua da Felicidade was like any other street in the Bazar. The windows of the *flower houses* remained shut, because their residents were fast asleep after the previous night's harvest. In the early afternoon, one could hear the clacking of mah-jong tablets and the plucking of string instruments as pupils set out on their apprenticeship to become sing-song girls. As evening fell, the lanterns were lit, and one by one, the houses were illuminated. That was when the sing-song girls, or *pei-pa-chais*, began to get dressed, to put on their carmine make-up, and perfume themselves. The fussiest among them spent hours in this ritual, surrounded by *mui-tchais* and the apprentices, who later on would become sing-song girls themselves.

Once darkness had fallen, the least sought after would go down and sit at the entrance, in groups, heavily made up, with flowers and ornaments in their hair, wearing brightly coloured gowns, fanning themselves and talking garrulously. Every few minutes, they would look surreptitiously at the street down which passed their potential clients. The well known ones, those with established reputations, remained in their rooms or played mah-jong or *tin-kao*, while they waited for messages summoning them to restaurants, hotels, and even private residences. Either that, or they would receive clients in their own rooms, something which was considered a special privilege.

In the golden age of the Bazar, there were no common prostitutes. It wasn't seen in a good light to sleep with a client on the first occasion, for this was shameful and cheap. Only after many meetings and much negotiation was such a favour granted. No one could oblige them to proceed in any other way, because their function was to sing. They were trained to perfection, to trill in falsetto long love songs, lamentations of yearning and sadness at separation, while at the same time plucking a lute or playing a string piano with a double bow made of the finest bamboo.

The apprentice, however, didn't limit herself to singing and learning the most subtle of practices in love. She went even further, for the sing-song girl had to learn to be essentially feminine and discreet in manner and conversation. She was taught poems, Confucian sayings, local legends, expressions of gentility and movements of the eyes and hands, all for the purpose of entertaining and seducing. In short, she possessed the most complete level of education in the art of pleasing. When she went out, she took with her an elderly maid, who would carry her string instrument, the mark of her profession. She would take a rickshaw if she was going further afield, or would walk when the destination was nearby. The *pei-pa-chais* of the Rua da Felicidade, were usually specially selected and bought when little from poverty stricken parents. If in many cases, their facial features did not coincide with western ideas of beauty, they were certainly pretty as far as the Chinese were concerned. The more oblique the eyes, the more salient the cheekbones, in other words the more oriental the face, the greater the value placed upon the girl. But whether they were beautiful or, in the eyes of some Europeans, ugly, they were all fragile and dainty, all knew how to laugh modestly, to walk with short, careful step, and to move their elegant, well kept hands and the rest of their body in suggestively erotic affectation. They possessed such refined manners that no one could ever feel ashamed in their company, and they were well known for the dignity of their behaviour.

Those who read the pages of writers and journalists who set down their impressions of Macau for posterity, will see that they were unanimous in paying homage to the charms of the *pei-pa-chais*.

Of course, such deceitfully glittering appearances concealed great tragedy, much suffering and cruelty. The sing-song girl, bought as a child, was practically a slave of her *madame*, who exploited her and kept all her earnings, even gifts from clients. If the *pei-pa-chai* didn't manage to purchase her freedom or become the concubine of a rich Chinese, she turned into a defenceless creature once her youth faded, for she could not survive in any other profession. She would leave the Rua da Felicidade, that consumer of women, and end up in the back lanes and alleyways, as exploited as ever. It was, after all, a harsh world, which was why suicide was not uncommon among sing-song girls.

I never knew the Rua da Felicidade during the halcyon days of the Bazar. I knew it during the war, when it already bore the mark of new times, when the *pei-pa-chai* was rapidly losing her professional status as a singer and degenerating into the condition of an expensive prostitute, who didn't bother to select her clients, just as long as they paid well. But there were still many *flower houses* that more or less stuck to the old traditions.

It was one such place that became associated with my recollections of Maurício, because of the following episode.

One freezing cold afternoon in December 1943, I was coming up the Avenida Almeida Ribeiro from the direction of the Largo de Hong Kong Mio, for some reason that escapes me. I was hunched up against the icy wind that blew against my back. There would have been nothing more welcome than to be able to eat a *ta-pin-lou*, or a bowl of snake soup, two winter dishes that are unsurpassed in Chinese cuisine. But my meagre earnings as a civil servant didn't allow me such luxuries, all the more so, with the prohibitive prices brought on by the war.

While crossing the icy blow hole of the Rua dos Mercadores, which joins the Avenida at the corner of the old Victoria Cinema, now the Tai Fung Bank, I suddenly ran into Maurício. Unlike me, he was well wrapped up in a new overcoat of an English cut, that gave him an air of refinement and prosperity. He let out one of those loud exclamations that were so typical of him, giving the other passers-by a fright.

He told me bluntly that I was the very person he wanted to see. He had an astounding piece of news to give me. He dragged me by the arm and we walked towards the *Golden Gate*, the well-known restaurant on the ground floor of the Hotel Central, which rivalled the Delícias at the Hotel Riviera in popularity.

The restaurant was packed at that hour. We went upstairs, but still had to stand waiting for a good ten minutes before a table became free in a corner, suitable for the exchange of confidences. I was dying of curiosity and Maurício could hardly contain what he wanted to get off his chest. We ordered coffee from the harassed waiter and Maurício blurted out the following:

"In the Felicidade, there's a virgin to be broken in."

I was perplexed by those words. What on earth did a virgin have to do with Maurício? I thought he was playing with me. But the feverish look in his eyes, the expression on his face of one who was living in the expectation of delight, convinced me he was serious and that he was about to tell me something unusual. He was amused by my surprise, and after the waiter had served us, he explained himself, noisily sipping the tasteless mixture that passed for coffee.

Early that afternoon, an *agent* had turned up in his office with the offer. In one of the *flower houses*, there was a girl who had just reached the age to start work. She was a sweet seventeen year-old, prepared ever since childhood to become a sing-song girl, a beautiful delicate young thing. As was the custom, the *madame* had spread the word around, inviting the highest bidder to have the privilege of deflowering her. The wretched woman had demanded one thousand five hundred *patacas*, of which only a tiny part would go to the poor girl, another to her natural parents, while she would keep the lion's share for herself. He had found the price too high, but it was still subject to negotiation. To make matters worse there was a Chinese, a collaborator with the Japanese, who was after the same prize. He didn't want it to go to an auction. Straight after coffee, he, Maurício, and the agent were going to pay the *madame* a visit in order to do some hard bargaining.

"Are you capable of doing such a thing?" I asked in dismay.

Maurício raised his eyebrows in surprise at such a question. He answered quite naturally:

"And why not? If I don't get there first, someone else will. That's for sure. I have the right to be with her for five days. I'll take her to my hideaway, and during that time, I shall be her *husband*. It's something new for me. I've never been with a virgin!"

He was so candid in his talk that I could only laugh. War had hardened me so that nothing surprised me. Maurício was practical in his hedonism, and he had none of the moral scruples I had. He mentioned there was another girl in the same situation in the Beco das Galinhas, but cheaper. I declined his offer.

"She's made of different clay. I only like fine porcelain, the type that tinkles."

Not long after, we got up when a cross-eyed little man with a sly look glanced over from the top of the stairs and waved to Maurício. I was invited to attend the negotiating session. I refused, but later regretted it, for I would have witnessed a unique scene. I said goodbye downstairs between gusts of wind, while Maurício promised solemnly to let me know the outcome of the affair.

Two days went by before I met my friend again enthusiastically rubbing his hands with glee. He had called me to his hideaway, discreetly situated in quiet rooms over in the direction of the Repouso road. He was very busy getting the house ready, especially the bedroom, where there was a huge bed covered in new linen sheets. He was behaving as if he were about to get married. He was indulging in such luxury, because he had plenty of money to spend. Long gone were the days of the little boy in short trousers, shivering with cold, climbing the Calçada do Tronco Velho to school. But I called him to task for the expense he was going to. He had even put new curtains in.

"My dear friend, it's the first time I've received a virgin here in this house and in this bed!"

He offered me a cigar and the remains of some whiskey – a very rare drink during the war – and his eyes still gleaming, told me that everything had gone to plan. The old shrew had asked for one thousand eight hundred *patacas*, in Macau currency, for the Hong Kong notes were worthless. She had raised the price because of that hideous collaborator, who, not happy with the three concubines he had locked away in his house, wanted to gobble up the girl. It had been a tough fight, which had required ranting and raving, followed by calm, and then gentle words.

He was very grateful to the *agent*. The poor devil had worked so hard, constantly coming and going, continually on the phone, thinking up strategies to soften the old woman's heart. For his services he had got a magnificent tip!

The bottom line was that the merchandise had to be genuine. He wasn't going to be tricked, to be sold a cat for a hare, no sir! But he hadn't gone as far as demanding a full examination before parting with his money. A mere introduction had satisfied him.

What he had seen left him infatuated. What a jewel, what hands, what gentle manners! Timid, downcast eyes, a touching shyness, a row of very white teeth, so clean! He was delighted and didn't hesitate for one moment. He couldn't face the possibility of some filthy collaborator being the first to taste such a heavenly dish. The sacrifice of a few more *patacas* was worth it, that was for sure! The old woman assured him that despite her chaste demeanour, she was well acquainted with all the secrets of love. He wouldn't shed tears over the money he had spent.

He told me all this as he bustled around getting everything ready. I didn't query his taste in decoration for fear of offending him. I thought the curtains, for example, horrible, as well as the loud red satin eiderdown. But maybe the bride would appreciate such tenderness.

Suddenly, he stopped and his expression became serious. He hesitated for a moment and then confided in me:

> "You're shocked by what I'm doing. It goes against everything we were taught. You think it's uncivilized, or it's too civilized for our way of seeing things. But listen… I couldn't bear not to tell you a secret I know you'll respect. In five days' time, I leave for Free China. I'm going to break the Japanese blockade, and I'm taking something important with me. Don't ask me what it is. I wouldn't tell you. The

risk is terrifying, I may die, but if I succeed, I'll earn a fortune. I want to take with me something wonderful from Macau to remember, something to comfort me on my journey. If I die, at least I'll go happy."

His expression changed as he invited me to the banquet. He was going to celebrate the girl's official entry into the world of prostitution in style, and he wanted to impress her. I thought he was going a bit too far and his gesture might be thought of as being in bad taste.

Nonsense! Came the answer. The *madame* was absolutely delighted. Such procedure was an honour, it demonstrated respect for her business and her *pei-pa-chai*. No, I couldn't miss it, and he would expect me at eight o'clock on the chosen day.

When I turned into the Rua da Felicidade on the evening of the banquet, it was crowded with people going this way and that, some striding purposefully along, pushing their way through without a care, others walked more slowly, as if uncertain which way to go. It was cold, but bearable now that the wind had dropped. Street vendors selling soup, dumplings and noodles, sadly plied their trade. Blind folk passed by with their lutes, ringing their bells, looking for customers to sing to. Most of the houses were gas lit, which cast a lurid glare round about. Beggars in rags – the most heart rending picture from those war years – mumbled their pathetic stories as they held out their skinny hands. Sadly, few people were moved, for most people remained indifferent to a scene that was all too familiar.

I passed various houses, from where crowds of girls peeped behind the glass door. Although the windows were closed, the clacking of mah-jong pieces could be heard, along with the tearful twanging of a string piano being played by some inspired sing-song girl. Steam wafting into the street from an eating house brought the unmistakable smell of dog meat being cooked.

Finally, I stopped in front of the house I was making for, and checked the number. Its front was similar to all the others, but it was one of the best in the whole quarter. The *flowers* were justly famous, selected by the cunning, discerning eye of the *madame*, a little woman with bound feet, who displayed an abundance of jade rings and bracelets, and welcomed her clients with a gold toothed smile. She was proud of her profession, she herself had once been a sing-song girl, and she boasted that her girls were brought up to be concubines for rich Chinese men. This was in large measure true. Many of them married and married well.

When I opened the door and went into the small entrance hall, an elderly maid bowed and showed me the stairs. The sudden change in temperature suddenly made me feel dizzy, especially when I was hit by the strong smell of sandalwood, which was being burned on the Buddhist altar, a feature of all the entrances to love houses. All along the wall in front of the stairs, there was a hard, wide divan made of dark wood, where the middle aged and elderly women, with their braids or top notches, sat. These women performed minor functions in that huge house, while the young ones were recruited up above.

The stairs creaked as I climbed them, aged by generations of men in search of escape. A little maid appeared from nowhere, and showed me the way.

On the first floor, I went down a corridor, on either side of which were little cubicles separated by walls or wooden partitions. Some had their doors barely shut, and women's faces and laughter could be seen and heard. The same smell of sandalwood followed me, now mixed with women's intoxicating perfumes.

At the end of the corridor, but on the street side, came the murmur of voices and the sound of mah-jong pieces. The whining notes of a lute accompanied the high-pitched voice of a sing-song girl. I stopped on the threshold of the large room where the banquet in honour of Maurício's virgin was going to be held.

Two round tables, each seating twelve people, had already been prepared. They were fully laid with bowls, little dishes and china spoons of the best type. Ivory chopsticks were set alongside the bowls and, in front, there were little round and square saucers with the sauces and condiments for each dish. No one was sitting at table yet. They were crowded to one side, round the tables for mah-jong, *sap-sam-cheong* or Russian poker. Almost all the *flowers* were fluttering round them like butterflies, with their laughter, their soothing voices and their stylised manners. There were others recruited from the house next door to ensure there were enough women for the invited guests. The sing-song girl who trilled her tune for a Chinese man, smoking as he sat there, seemed totally unperturbed in her duties.

I felt intimidated when all I saw were Chinese faces. Then I caught sight of Maurício coming towards me. He radiated the happiness of a real bridegroom. Behind him came Leonel, an old classmate from the Lycée, who was now in trade and a close associate of Maurício's in wartime business. We were the only Portuguese there, the others being newly rich, prosperous Chinese. Being a friend of Maurício's, I was treated kindly by everyone.

The same young maid who had led me into the room, now offered me a hot scented towel. I had hardly wiped my hands when another servant offered me a dish of tea. It was my favourite type, *heong pin*. I sipped it keenly, and only then did the first maid give me a tin of cigarettes. The second one proffered a light, as if she were competing with the other girl in matters of courtesy.

I began to relax, exchanging pleasantries here and there. Two *flowers* came up to me on either side. They hadn't yet found a master for the banquet. They weren't particularly pretty, but they looked stupendously classy in their tight fitting cheongsams, with the daring slit up the side. They waved their fans, more as an instrument of seduction than of any practical use, shook their handkerchiefs, and fell over themselves in their attentions.

Maurício came over again. There was no doubt about it, he was the king of the party. He dispensed the honours, cruising round the room like the perfect host and answering all the mischievous comments. All was laughter round about him.

"Where's the girl?"

"She's inside, decorating herself like a bride. She's a peach. You'll see…"

At that moment, the attention of those in the room was drawn to the poker table, where play was turning tough and bad-tempered, while the bank had to bear the brunt of ever more extravagant bets. When the cards were turned up, there was always uproar among the men, while the women discussed their mistakes, pretending to be annoyed or to praise intelligent combinations. As I wasn't playing, I just looked on. The two *flowers* fluttered around me, waiting for me to make my choice.

The *madame* came in with quick childlike steps in her bound feet. She was leaning on a *mui-tchai*, eight years old and heavily made up, who had clearly begun her apprenticeship as a future *pei-pa-chai*. In her fluted, childish voice, she invited everybody to make themselves at home, and asked Maurício to be patient. As for me, she asked me in florid terms whose meaning I managed to grasp, whether I had made my choice, and she pointed to the two *flowers*. Before I could answer, Maurício pushed the one on the left towards me and, as a connoisseur, told me she was the best.

"Don't worry… Everything's paid for."

The one on the right disappeared discreetly, with neither a word nor gesture of disappointment.

We sat in a corner, and she began to serve me. She changed the tea in my dish, and it remained replenished for the rest of the night, she pointed out various brands of rice wine, in the absence of other alcoholic drinks that had been made scarce by the war.

We started a polite and conventional conversation. The girl, who was in her early twenties, still fresh and in her girlish prime, fired me with kind and considerate questions. It was as if no other man existed for her at that moment. When she smiled, she placed her fan in front of her mouth, and laughed quietly, for it was not considered good taste to laugh out loud. She did everything to please, while doing so without apparent effort. Unfortunately, my Chinese was from the streets, which meant that I could not return her carefully chosen words in kind. But she understood me, and that was what was important.

In that enclosed space, the smell of cigarettes mixed with that of Filipino cheroots, obtained goodness knows how, and suddenly the winter wind blowing outside seemed far away. As if she realized that I was about to start sweating, my *flower*, funnelling her hands, began to cool me with her fan. Pampered and comfortable, I was beginning to forget what I had come for.

The *madame*'s childlike voice suddenly echoed, asking us to stop our mah-jong and poker because dinner was served. Accounts were settled and we all got up to go to the tables for the banquet.

As if conforming to some strict etiquette, at that very moment, the figure of Maurício's virgin candidate for prostitution appeared at the door. There was a brief silence as all our attention was directed towards her.

In came the *bride*! She was dressed in a handsome red silk cheongsam, which hugged her, throwing into relief the curves of her slim body. She had a pretty oriental face, with almond eyes and salient cheekbones. She was certainly not of peasant background. She would have been more beautiful if she hadn't been plastered with carmine, but red was part and parcel of the occasion. Her wavy hair fell onto her shoulders, as if she had come straight from the hairdresser's. She moved forward with coquettish grace, and with a light and elegant step.

Although Maurício had exaggerated somewhat, I had to agree with him. The girl was fascinating. Her whole being pulsated at that crucial moment in her life, when she knew how important first impressions were. From that night on, she would rise in the ranking of her world and achieve equality with the others. Her small breasts heaved, heightened by the clever cut of her gown. She was happy, confident of her beauty and youth, slipping among the guests who honoured her. She displayed modesty, but at the same time, and this was part of the mystery of the *pei-pa-chais*, she left behind her a trace of eroticism that was hard to describe.

The *madame* surveyed her work. All that money used to buy and educate her had not been spent in vain.

Her long hours of teaching, during which there had been no shortage of beating and other tortuous punishment, had produced a result that exceeded all expectations. And the sale of her virginity for a good price partly compensated her for all her cares.

Maurício, unable to control himself, violated the subtleties of protocol, as he seized the girl's hands and tried to raise them to his lips. In such refined Chinese surroundings, his attitude was not only uncalled for, but in bad taste. She resisted by skilfully avoiding him. But she gave him a smile as if to forgive him his lapse.

The chairs were pulled out and the men sat down. The women sat down behind, as tradition demanded, each of them serving the guest to whom she had been assigned. They did not take part in the banquet, none of them were there to eat their fill, but rather to entertain. Even the virgin had no more privileges than the others, merely doing what they did but for Maurício.

The dishes began to appear one after the other, brought in by the maids. None of the men used their chopsticks to pick the pieces of food directly from the steaming dishes. This was the job of the *pei-pa-chais*, who took the food and placed it in the little bowls, from where the men, in turn, took it and ate it. In this way, the ceremony proceeded according to its own set of rules. While they served us diligently and ever watchfully, the women also kept filling our glasses with the powerful rice wine. They cooled us with their fans and only ate anything when we pressed them, and even then, only an occasional morsel. This was undoubtedly a world where men prevailed!

I can't recall all the dishes that were brought to the table at regular intervals, but they were all worthy representatives of the rich Cantonese cuisine. I remember the black eggs accompanied by slices of ginger, shark's fin soup, fried grouper in sweet sauce, swallow's nest broth, frogs' legs, turtle, quails' eggs and a roast suckling pig, which is a sign of virginity.

Maurício, ignoring convention, regaled his companion with tenderness and attention. He whispered things to the girl, who never lost her composure even though she was often embarrassed by his exuberant behaviour towards her. As for the rest of the people, it was more like a smart gathering than a party in a brothel. In fact, this was a point of honour in the *flower houses* of the Rua da Felicidade, which maintained their tradition. According to Chinese social conventions of the time, lasciviousness only occurred behind closed doors, in the intimacy of the bedroom.

Under the influence of the wines that kept flowing, and all the more so because of the never ending succession of toasts, the guests began to talk loudly, their faces flushed. They began to make saucy comments with a hidden meaning, which the women returned in kind, in an entertaining duel full of elaborate phrases that were incomprehensible to me. It was a form of flirtation that was beyond the understanding of the European, more blunt and pragmatic in his approach, but which slowly paved the way for the delights that awaited in bed.

In order to force Maurício to drink more, they challenged him to *fat-choi*, a complicated game of words and finger gestures, which was played to song. Whoever lost, had to drink half or the entire contents of the glasses. Maurício was an expert at the game, just like any native Chinese, and almost always won, making everyone laugh hilariously and the virgin he was going to deflower all the more proud.

Some time after eleven, the last course was served, by which time I had lost count of them all. As was the custom, everyone got up, belching with satisfaction. For Maurício who could hardly contain his impatience, despite his generosity as a host, it was a relief. Half the men left, after the usual expressions of gratitude. The girls who were free also withdrew to attend to other commitments in hotels and restaurants.

Not long afterwards, Maurício and his virgin left in the rickshaws that had been waiting outside for some time. I shook him warmly by the hand, for I wasn't going to see him until he returned from his mysterious journey. It might even be the last time I would have the privilege of enjoying his company. I allowed myself to stay on, enjoying the comforts of that house, and listening to the doleful tones of the girl who had served me, as she sang to me and played her string piano...

About a month later, Maurício phoned me. He was back, safe and sound. He had left and returned by mysterious routes, without losing so much as a thread of hair. I met up with him and Leonel in his discreet hideaway. I found him sunburnt and brimming with health. He was exhilarated by his adventure, more convinced than ever that he had been blessed by luck. We talked about all sorts of things, but never about the real reasons for his journey.

It was natural that after a while our conversation should turn to that famous night in the Felicidade. Maurício's expression changed to one of genuine fascination. He exalted the five days he had spent with Yao Man, as a time when he had experienced the most complete happiness. Knowing he was going on a journey during which he might die, he had excelled in his tenderness and behaved as he never had done before with any other woman. Although he must have guessed our insatiable curiosity, he didn't descend into detail, as if knowledge of his intimate moments was to be his alone. We respected his gentlemanly discretion, even though we found it unlike him. But he couldn't resist heaping praise on the girl's caresses, the gentle smoothness of her delicate hands.

> "You know how I tend to get headaches, especially down towards the back of my neck. The very next day, sure enough, I had one. I thought I was going to die, but Yao Man, caring as ever, began to massage me. Oh! How her hands worked wonders! She held my head, moved it from side to side. I swear I heard a crack at the top of my spine, and then she

slowly rubbed the back of my neck with her fingers."

"And what about the headache?"

"It went away, and hasn't been back since. I know where to get a cure any time I need treatment."

He lit a cigarette to better appreciate our astonishment. Then, taking his time, he confided in us further:

"And she had another secret…"

We lent forward anxiously. Maurício, enraptured, murmured:

"She bathed me in tea… Do you know what it's like?"

"No!"

"Well, give it a try. It was a warm, aromatic tea, delightful! I asked her what tea it was. She smiled and told me it was just an ordinary sort… But I don't believe it. I came out clean, smelling good and later, how ardent I was!"

He sat gazing at the wall, in ecstasy at the memory of it. Leonel and I began to wonder what the mysterious aphrodisiac in that strange bath might have been.

"That's a good one… It could only happen to Maurício. Nothing like that has ever come my way," Leonel complained bitterly.

"Ask your wife to give you one."

Leonel shrugged his shoulders in disappointment, and we took our leave of Maurício, with our thoughts on tea and neck massages.

I found myself in Maurício's company on a number of other occasions, but during the last year of the war, he was always busy. In my routine as a civil servant, I moved in circles that were of no interest to him. We met infrequently, and weeks would go by when we didn't see each other.

As for Yao Man, I would occasionally catch sight of her, passing by in a rickshaw, or getting out of a car in the company of rich Chinese men, at the door of the Hotel Central. After her initiation with Maurício, she was very much sought after. Whenever we passed each other, she would always give me a warm smile. Once or twice, I saw her with my friend.

One day, on one of the rare occasions when he could spare me a few minutes, he summed up his impressions of Yao Man:

> "She's happy. Those five days were a great honour for her. When she returned to the Felicidade, she had tears in her eyes. I was touched, too... what a girl! She thanked me and superstitiously told me I had brought her luck. She's made a good career for herself in her line of business. She's always in demand. The *madame* looks after her with special care. She enjoys her work because she was never taught to do anything else. But with me, it's not work. She's herself. I was, after all, the first one, and that's stayed. Maurício knows a thing or two! She complains I don't see her enough. If only I could, but you know me, with all my commitments. But in spite of everything, I've got a monopoly of two things: the tea bath and the neck massages. She swears she doesn't do that with anyone else."

"And do you believe her?"

"Yes, I do," he replied with total conviction.

One day, I asked Leonel if he had tried a tea bath. He looked at me peevishly and said:

> "Those things only happen to lucky devils like Maurício. When I suggested it to my wife, she couldn't believe what she was hearing and shouted: 'That's all I needed! Are you drunk?'"

He seemed so out of sorts that I didn't pursue the matter.

In August 1945, the peace that we all yearned for arrived. Church bells rang out, prayers of thanksgiving could be heard, fire crackers were let off, the whole city was lit up in celebration. Those were euphoric days, when everyone talked about a new age of redemption and prosperity. Maurício once again emigrated to Hong Kong and the following July, I set off for Coimbra. I navigated my way through university, with ups and downs in my studies, and eight years later returned to Macau, where I became a lawyer. During my long absence, I wrote just one letter to my friend, but never got an answer.

Two years after my return, on one of my visits to Hong Kong, I came across his address quite by chance. When I phoned him, the roar he let out at the other end of the line was deafening. I invited him to lunch, and we met on the rooftop of the Gloucester Hotel, now no more, a quiet, comfortable place in the style of an English club, such as one seldom finds nowadays in Hong Kong.

Maurício had put on a bit of weight, but he was still the same. He bombarded me with questions, and I gave as good as I got. In a nutshell, Maurício was living in Hong Kong, and had a small trading firm, and while he was not as rich as at the end of the war, he was beginning to prosper again.

"I lost a lot of money in stupid ventures. I was almost penniless when the Korean War began. I was in that pigsty at Pusan, and managed to claw back some money. Don't ask what I got myself into. But you can imagine… Now I'm in Hong Kong, taking advantage of this boom, which is changing the whole face of the city."

"Did you never go back to Macau?"

"Never again. I like vibrant, dynamic cities. I miss it, who wouldn't? But Macau is too small for me."

"Are you still single?"

"Inverately so. I'm not a man for marriage… The only time I had something approaching family life were those five days with Yao Man. Do you remember her? After her, never again. The life I lead doesn't chime in with bedroom slippers and children. I don't have a fixed home. At the moment I'm in Hong Kong, but tomorrow I might be in Singapore or Saigon or anywhere else where there's a whiff of money."

"Do you only ever think of money?"

"I was very poor when I was a child and growing up," he said, with candour.

"What's happened to Yao Man?"

"She got married. She's the third wife of a rich Chinese. She lives right here in Kowloon, in a beautiful house. When the brothels closed in the Felicidade, she moved to Hong Kong with the *madame*. The rich Chinese paid a good price to free her. The old shrew wouldn't accept anything less. Now she's his favourite. She came to me for advice before taking the plunge, because I never let her out of my sight during all these years. I told her she'd better look after herself because youth doesn't last forever. Besides, the age of the *pei-pa-chais* was finished. I wouldn't have relished the thought of seeing her passing from one to another, down the line. She listened to me."

"Did she keep her promise?"

"What promise?"

Then he remembered and answered me forcefully:

"Ah, the promise about the tea? Of course she kept it and still does. Don't forget, I was the first. Why would she waste her time now on a fat old man, covered in flab and, besides, beyond arousal?"

He swallowed his whiskey, and indicated to the waiter that he wanted another one. After a brief silence, he added in a strangely melancholic tone:

"I could do with some massages on the back of my neck. But she doesn't give me them anymore, because she's become a proper wife, for one man only…"

For the first time, I sensed he was jealous, But it was something he would never have admitted, he who claimed to have a heart of concrete. What he was forgetting was that even concrete gets cracks.

He remained abroad, and I stayed in Macau, so we lost contact with each other. I heard at one point that he had left for Indochina, where a new war had broken out. The old rogue never wrote to me. Only once, round about Christmas time, some ten years ago, a packet of cigars arrived for me through the post, some magnificent Filipino Coronas, each one with my name on its label. A simple card, with the following message, accompanied the gift: *Fond regards from Maurício*. There wasn't even an address to which I could send my thanks.

In 1968, I went to Japan and Korea. One afternoon, in Tokyo, I was strolling down the Ginza, killing time before going to the Kabuki. I had arrived there from Nikko and I still had in my mind the vision of the cherry trees and cedars that abound in that dreamlike sanctuary. The whole avenue was buzzing with the rumble of traffic and crowds of people. With the eyes of a tourist, pausing here and there, I took in the mighty beat of a huge capital city.

Suddenly, I stopped in my tracks, startled. I heard my name being called, turned and found myself in Maurício's bear hug. He looked extremely well, as if the years were having no effect on him at all. Maurício, with his hearty laugh and his warm geniality, was the last person I expected to meet in the middle of the Ginza. His thumps on the back all but crushed my bones.

The circumspect Japanese gave us a wide berth, a haughty Englishman dropped his pipe, in the face of this Portuguese expansiveness.

"You… in Japan?"

"So you can see! In flesh and blood. I've been here a couple of years now and spend my time between Taipei and Tokyo. I'm working with the Americans."

Hardly had I recovered from my surprise than I saw the beautiful Yao Man standing beside me. She was now somewhat matronly, but still slender, in her cheongsam with its audacious opening. She recognized me and smiled. And clinging to her, two little ones, a clever looking little boy of five, and a bashful little girl of two, with profoundly oriental eyes, but her father's nose and mouth.

"Here's my family!"

I shook Yao Man by the hand, and fondled the children's faces. The parents invited me to dinner. Sadly, I had to decline. I was going to the Kabuki with some Japanese friends and was leaving for Seoul the following day. I promised to look them up on my return from Korea. All this was arranged in the heart of the noisy Ginza, he giving his word he would be waiting for me at the airport.

Then Yao Man, guessing that we wanted to talk alone for a few moments, went off to look at the shop windows with the children.

"I still can't believe it!," I exclaimed."

"You've got to. It all began during those five days. It was then that we both had the happiest moments of our lives. We never forgot. We understood each other despite our different education and customs. I didn't take anything seriously, she was in awe of her profession. We were too young to realize that life could be any different. We said goodbye as friends, but we always tried to be with each other whenever we could. She got tired of what she did, and became a rich man's concubine. He gave her jewels, a house and a Cadillac, but never gave her a home. The two children she had by the man, goodness knows how, were never able to call her mother. As you know, a concubine's children always regard the first wife as their mother. This made her bitter. I wandered this world and ended up in Saigon. I prospered, but one day, as I was leaving a cinema, a bomb went off. I looked death in the face and lay in a hospital for months. I lost all my illusions. My life was pointless and I was horrified by the idea of dying, my body rotting away in some field, with no one to mourn me."

He arched his eyebrows and stroked his chin as he remembered.

> "During my sleepless nights, I began to yearn for those fingers that used to stroke my neck. I went back to Hong Kong and found Yao Man, alone and widowed, her husband conveniently dead and buried, her children living with the first wife, as the only male heirs to continue the family line. We felt we couldn't waste any more time playing with fate. We decided to re-live those five days, and they've continued to this day. We got married, moved to Japan, and the little ones were born. Now I'm the one with the slippers. That's it…"

I congratulated him heartily. The kids were clamouring for their father. Yao Man still waited, smiling. We said goodbye with another Portuguese hug. I still had one more question to ask him, but I was embarrassed. She walked away again, but turned to laugh.

> "I know what it is you want to ask. Go on… feel free."

> "Does she still…?"

> "She does… That was another thing that brought me back. She still bathes me with that special tea, but now, it also has essence of cherry."

He gave me a generous wave and went off to join his family. The sound of his laughter hovered over the length of the Ginza as he disappeared with his loved ones among the crowd.

CANDY

He had arrived in Hong Kong on the ten o'clock hydrofoil in the company of just one friend. The journey had taken place in bright sunshine, over a sea as smooth as velvet. A Chinese was waiting for them on the jetty, to take his luggage to Kai Tak. His friend's kindness had made life easier and left him free until it was time to go to the airport. His flight to Brazil, by way of the United States, only left at night.

> "Don't worry about your luggage. A-Chun will take care of everything and will be there waiting to pick it up. I'm sorry I can't go with you. I have to return to Macau at noon."

> "Until Brazil then, or Macau… or some other place in the world."

They said goodbye. A quick hug to avoid any emotion, and they wished each other happiness amid the general indifference of the crowd around them. Biting his lip, he waved one last time and then watched his friend disappear in a private car.

He wondered where to go, and then gradually left the area of the quay, heading for the centre of the city along Des Voeux Road. Here he was greeted by the intense rumble of traffic, mingling with the packed crowd of passers-by, hurrying along, each one making for his own particular destination.

He walked the length of one block, without being attracted by anything he saw in the shop windows. He saw a free taxi and hailed it. He decided to go to Kowloon, crossing the harbour on the ferry so as to enjoy one of the most beautiful sights in the world.

"Star Ferry."

How he missed Macau having left it. He could still feel his friend's warm embrace. He felt a vague need to cry. Two weeks in his homeland after an absence of twenty-four years had hardly been enough. It would have been better if he hadn't come back. But how could a Macanese turn down the chance of seeing his homeland again when given the opportunity?

His mind was still full of the sights of his native city. The trees along the Praia Grande and the Chunambeiro, the mellow autumn sunset watched from one of the belvederes on the Penha hill, the Meia-Laranja, with the sight of its junks eternally coming and going from the fishing grounds, the streets and alleyways, wending their way down from S. Lourenço to Manduco beach, the narrow and twisting residue of an old Macau now tending to disappear.

He had made full use of his stay. He had satisfied his long craving for Macanese and Chinese food, savoured with their own local ingredients, he had enjoyed the sincere hospitality of his friends, had tenderly deposited a wreath on his parents' grave and visited the school where, as a young boy he had dreamed of wider horizons and distant places.

He had been shocked by the changing face of his city. There were new districts, modern blocks and seething traffic. That was progress, people said. The early 1970s were years of optimism and a promise of new prosperity. There was the future bridge, the new Hotel Lisboa, tourists in their droves and many other things, whose novelty was beginning to shake the sleepy old town from its lethargy.

Two weeks had been enough to acquaint him with the latest intrigues, rumours and gossip. In these things Macau hadn't changed. He discovered a new restaurant, the Solmar, where he could meet his friends of old. He had found out who had died, and who had left for distant lands. He had brought himself up to date with Macau and its news.

The taxi braked suddenly and he was awakened from his daydreams. He paid, got out and wandered leisurely over to the newspaper stand. He bought a paper and with the same unhurried air strolled over to one of the many snaking queues of passengers waiting to be allowed onto the jetty to board the ferries.

He looked around distractedly. In front of him, a typical Englishman, dressed as elegantly as if he were in Regent Street, was reading his paper, three American sailors shouted rowdy jokes that only they understood, a German woman scolded her naughty child. Behind him, an Indian woman in a brightly coloured sari and a red dot on her forehead, clutched her shopping as if scared they might be stolen, and two Chinese women, dressed in European manner, talked together in Mandarin.

He glanced over at the other queues in a similarly casual way. The bustle was ceaseless, from morning till night. Then he was suddenly struck with astonishment. That slender woman over there in the farthest queue, so well dressed and with such elegant shoes, with an air of such splendid opulence, was Candy without a shadow of doubt. He hadn't seen her in person for twenty-four years, and there she was, as fascinating as ever, with her aristocratic air, amid the mass of anonymous folk.

He knew she was in Hong Kong, and without pushing his inquiries, had heard what had happened to her. She had done well for herself, marrying an Englishman from the cream of colonial society. Her face often appeared on the social pages of the press, at charity events and cocktail parties given by the diplomatic community. There had even been a long article about her house, perched high up on the Peak, in an exclusive area, with photographs of her lounge, dining room and the garden. In Spring, her flowering azaleas and chrysanthemums were famous.

On the other hand, most people found her unpleasant. Her husband's position had gone to her head, she looked down on her family and had cut herself off from her own folk and friends of old, ensconced as she was among the English. In short, Candy felt nothing for those she had left behind.

He had assumed Candy to be no more than a figure from the past, reduced to the cold ashes of memory. But there she was once more, a mere stone's throw away, as if produced for him by the arts of a magician with a taste for the ironic, and he felt his pulse racing, as if all his senses had been reawakened.

His first impulse was to slip away unnoticed. This was no longer the Candy of past times, but the distinguished Mrs Morris-White. And then there was that whole business of the night when they had last met.

He buried his face in his paper, paid for his ticket, took some time getting his change, much to the impatience of those behind him and then took up a position in front of an advertisement for typewriters.

Candy moved forward, climbed the stairs and with casual elegance walked down to the end of the corridor. He watched her as she walked away from him. He calculated that she must be about forty-five. But she was very well kept, and didn't look more than thirty-six or thirty-seven. Like a doe in her prime, her hips rolled in gentle rhythm, and with her long legs, like those of a model, she moved with confidence and self-assurance. Her waist was no longer so narrow, but had thickened sensuously.

Not once did she look back. Like a meteor, she appeared suddenly before him only to disappear again. And he would never know by what mysterious means she had married so fabulously well.

This was truly amazing for when he had first come across her some twenty-seven years before, she was a poor war refugee who had fled Hong Kong under occupation and sought shelter in Macau, pale and hungry, with an old coat that barely covered her.

He met her a year later. It happened one cold night, in a bar selling sweet broth on the Rua do Campo, one of the many that existed there during the war years. He had gone there for supper with two friends after a trip to the cinema. When sitting down at a table, his attention was drawn to a group of war refugees. Among them was Candy.

He was interested in her, not only because she was pretty, but because of the avid way she drank her bowl of peanut broth and tore into a fritter. She was clearly ravenous. The honey from the fritter ran down the corner of her mouth, and the syrupy liquid made her lips shine.

He stared at her dark face, her sensual mouth and the pert curve of her breasts. After a while, the two groups fell into conversation with each other. They began to talk like old friends. His gaze lit up when he addressed the girl and she, with a mischievous laugh, sensed his interest. She gave the impression of being ready and willing to embark on some magnificent adventure.

She understood Portuguese, but answered him in studiously correct English. She had been an exceptionally good pupil at the Maryknolls convent school and the nuns had corrected her accent. As a Portuguese from Hong Kong, she naturally knew Macanese *patois*, but refused to speak it as she couldn't express herself in proper Portuguese. She had her pride.

They arranged to meet a few nights later, at a party to be held at one of the refugee centres. According to information received, she was a girl of lax morals, who had been raped by Japanese soldiers a few days after the surrender of Hong Kong. His first impression of her seemed to have been confirmed. He drove himself crazy thinking of ways to conquer her. The girl had a whole crowd of boys in tow, but favoured none of them in particular. She distributed smiles to them all, but nothing more. He only managed to dance with her three times.

Some time later, she favoured him with a stroll along the Avenida da República. They spent some time watching the fishermen pulling in their nets at Bom Parto and then sat on a bench chatting, and listening to the murmur of the sea under the cliff at Santa Sancha. They were two happy hours, her face relaxed, free from the stigma of war and poverty. Her smile sparkled spontaneously, ever mischievous.

She appeared level headed and businesslike. She told him the war had taught her one thing. She had suffered great hunger, and if she were to marry, it would be with a rich man. At that time, having just completed military service, and got a lowly paid job in a commercial firm, the meaning of her words was clear. And clearer still when she added:

"A woman shouldn't sell herself cheaply. She should know how to get the best possible deal."

In the days that followed, they became ever closer. They were mutually attracted by a fellow feeling. But she seemed to be denying her reputation. She allowed him to take her arm, and to kiss her. But she avoided any further intimacy.

At a lively dance held at the Melco Club, famous for its large parties during the war, he surprised her at her most voluptuous, languid and flirtatious. It was hot in the packed room, where more than a hundred couples were constantly turning round the dance floor. They had both drunk some concoction or other, in which there was a good measure of Chinese chicken feet, always guaranteed to go to the head of those not used to it. At a certain point he invited her to go for a walk in the garden.

There, amid the soothing scent of hyacinth, they walked towards the tennis courts, and then turned in the direction of the hippodrome. The moonlight and the aromas of the night went to their head. On all sides they could hear the crickets, screeching their strange courting song or something similar. There seemed to be a halo of light round Candy's face, and the perfume of her hair was disturbing. Suddenly they were in each other's arms, sliding to the ground, and making torrid love on the soft grass under a porch.

Much later, they got to their feet. She tried to smooth her crumpled skirt and tidy her hair, while he, tightening his belt, shook the dust from his trousers. They walked back amid the ceaseless song of the crickets, each one lost in their own thoughts.

"We did something crazy," said Candy.

"It was bound to happen sooner or later."

"Don't worry. We won't have a baby."

Those words, uttered so naturally, hurt more than they provided relief. They were the product of a mentality moulded by the cold practicalities of war.

They climbed the steps to the club and went into the lounge. They were playing *Moonlight Serenade*, a tune that he would forever associate with Candy. They danced cheek to cheek, their bodies entwined. She refused a whole queue of boys who wanted to dance with her, and whispered:

"Today, I'm all yours…"

"Only today?"

"Yes… What we did doesn't mean there's any commitment between us. Do you hear?"

"Yes, I do…"

The sound of rushing feet brought him back to reality. Candy was now far ahead of him. He would have to hurry if he was going to catch the same ferry. He stopped at the back of the packed crowd of passengers waiting for the iron gate to open.

The sun shone on Candy's brown hair. There she was, standing serenely at the head of the queue, without ever looking back, distinguished from the impatient crowd round about. Yet he was afflicted by one anguished question. Had she seen him? And was it right, after twenty-four years that she should be unaware of their being on the same ferry?

He followed the mass of human beings down the metal

gangplank once the gate had opened. He was absorbed for a few seconds by the clatter of feet. He jumped aboard the ferry, and looked for a seat opposite Candy, but two rows ahead, and pretended not to notice.

The bulky vessel began to move smoothly, completing an efficient manoeuvre with another ferry that was waiting to take its berth. He inhaled the autumn breeze that ruffled the green waters of the sea. And gazing at the wide vista of the harbour, he felt the same awe he had felt as a child.

As far as one could see there were liners, freighters and tankers of various nationalities scattered about moored to buoys, some working up a head of steam, others lying languidly in the sun. Around them, barges, pontoons and other craft loaded and unloaded freight, provisions, oil and water. Cranes creaked, working ceaselessly, amid the strident howls of hooters and sirens. To starboard loomed the grey shapes of American warships recently arrived from Vietnam. Everywhere, skimming over the choppy green waters, there were junks, yachts, launches, gasoline carriers, the so-called *walla-wallas*, tourist boats, hydrofoils from Macau and the ferries, all adding to the vibrancy of a booming port city.

Kowloon was growing. A 707 made its screaming descent towards Kai Tak. Nearby, a helicopter seemed to be hanging motionless in the air. In the distance, the black smoke from factories smudged the limpid backdrop of the sky.

He thought about Candy again. They kept their promise, they remained uncommitted to each other. It was easier like that, both enjoying themselves in that strange situation of war, which lent people a new personality. As for the future, no one could be sure, which was why people lived for the present. For three months, they shared more than a few moments of pleasure, especially when he managed to borrow a friend's house over towards the Estrada do Repouso. Then he lost her.

A rival entered the fray in the form of a Filipino who was mixed up in wartime business dealings, and flaunted his wealth. He had everything with which to seduce a girl keen to turn her back on poverty and avid for money. At first, he didn't suspect anything when she failed to turn up to their meetings. But then he became alarmed when he noticed the foreigner's attentions towards her. And to make matters worse, he was good looking.

It was then that he realized he was serious about her after all, and that she was no longer someone with whom to merely pass the time. He loved her and wanted her for himself. They began to have arguments that soured the atmosphere, and they would part disconsolately. One day, he insisted on her meeting him for tea at the Golden Gate, where he would introduce her to his parents. She refused but eventually gave in, more tired than willing. He waited an hour and a half for her, having to bear his parents' silent sympathy, but she didn't turn up.

Afterwards, he wandered aimlessly along the streets, blind with anger and humiliation. When he turned the corner by the Riviera, from where he could hear the unmistakable tones of Art Carneiro playing at a tea dance, he caught a glimpse of her through one of the windows, dancing in the rich man's intimate embrace.

He felt insulted, as if he had received the lash of a whip, but he had the good sense to control himself. She was living in the Clube de Macau, which had been turned into a refugee centre. He waited for her on the steps of the Santo Agostinho Church, opposite the club, for a last talk. She arrived just as the church bells were ringing for evening mass. He was planning to recite a rosary of complaints, but all he managed to utter were three or four harsh words. Irritated, she replied:

"I made it quite clear there was no commitment between us."

He shouted some rude remark by way of reply and turned on his heel. He stopped talking to her. Every time he saw her, though, he murmured to himself "I'll get my revenge". Once they almost bumped into each other in the street. He sensed that Candy was smiling at him, but he turned his face scornfully away.

The war ran its course and at last, in August 1945, the Japanese were beaten. Almost immediately, the refugees began their exodus to Hong Kong. A month and a half after the end of hostilities, he was standing on the quay of the Inner Harbour, saying goodbye to friends, when he caught sight of Candy among hundreds of passengers on the old steamer. She looked beautiful in her red dress. She was looking at him but he was still hurt and showed no forgiveness. He stood there impassively, as if she didn't exist, all the more so when the Filipino haughtily took her hand.

The following summer, there was the incident on that unforgettable night. But that's another story.

In Brazil and the United States, other affairs and other horizons eventually reduced the image of Candy to little more than a recollection. He consigned her to memory along with the many other episodes he experienced as a man. Now, it seemed, all that remained for him to discover was how she had managed such an extraordinary marriage to the Englishman.

The huge shape of an aircraft carrier attracted his attention for a few minutes. He leafed through his newspaper without reading anything in particular, took out a cigarette and inhaled deeply. Then he turned round.

Candy was looking at him.

There was a slight hesitation and then it all happened quite naturally. She recognized him, and they smiled at each other. After a period of twenty-four years, all passions had been spent. Any other attitude would have been absurd. He got up and apologizing as he went, picked his way past the other passengers.

"Hello…"

"Candy…"

They shook hands, as if they had always kept up their friendship. He was sure Candy was recalling that night in Repulse Bay. He sat down in an empty seat next to hers, and they talked in English.

Candy's English! How polished it was, with a true British accent, and liberal repetitions of "Oh, my goodness!" If one couldn't see her face, one would assume she was English through and through. It was effortless: she didn't need to act it up, or as they say in Macau, she didn't toast her English. She spoke it naturally, just as she had the natural refinement of a lady. Hardly surprising! Living in those social circles, how could she fail to adopt their own airs?

Now he was able to admire her from close quarters. How good looking she was in her mature, well groomed beauty, her hair without so much as a thread of grey, the work of an expensive hairdresser, her brown skin still smooth! She was dazzling! Among all those fair-haired English, her Macanese features would surely stand out.

"I had a feeling it was you when I got out of the car! I lost sight of you and thought I must have mixed you up with someone else. There are always lots of people waiting for the ferry. In fact, I don't look at people very much. When I saw you sit down in front of me, I knew it was you."

"I recognized you in the queue."

"So why didn't you come over?"

"Well…"

"And you mean you would have gone off goodness knows where without even saying hello."

"I didn't know how you'd take it."

She pursed her lips as if to reprimand him, but then she gave him that smile that reminded him of the Candy he had made love to on the grass at the Hippodrome.

She was burning with curiosity. What was he doing in Hong Kong? He told her. She raised her eyebrows in surprise. Brazil? That was somewhere she had always wanted to visit, but had never had the chance. Every summer, she went to Europe for her holidays, to the UK, with brief stops in the United States and Canada. But she had never set foot anywhere in the southern hemisphere.

After another question, he explained. This was his first visit back to the East after nearly a quarter of a century. How Macau and Hong Kong had both changed. What did he do in Brazil? He was an executive with an airline. That was why he'd hardly had to pay anything for the flight.

"You look magnificent! A bit older, you've put on a bit of weight, but apart from that you're the same as ever."

"As ever is too kind a way of putting it. I've got less hair, and I can't get rid of my paunch."

"Nonsense! You're still a lady-killer."

"And you! You're prettier than ever!"

"You flatter me. It's so nice of you to say so. But you forget I'm nearly fifty. I feel old."

"But you've got a good few years to go still. If that is being old, then no woman should fear it."

Kind words, ridiculous in tone, which masked their intense desire to know about the course each other's lives had taken.

"How long are you going to be in Hong Kong?"

"Not long. I leave at eight o'clock tonight."

"So soon? What a pity. But are you free until then?"

"Yes, I'm just wandering around, here and there, and down memory lane."

"I'm free too. My husband has gone to Lantao and only gets back tonight. I've got no commitments, except to say goodbye to two friends at Kai Tak. Do you want to come with me?"

"Of course, I'd like that very much. I'd regret it for the rest of my life if I didn't say yes."

"Then, lets go…"

"Let me invite you to lunch."

"That would be nice."

Some days before, she added, she had had a problem with the car. This was now ready and would be in one of the car parks behind the Peninsula Hotel, as she had instructed. She was on her way to pick it up and after Kai Tak, she would take him for a drive.

When the ferry tied up at the terminal in Kowloon, they left side by side, the rhythm of the crowd forcing them to walk quickly. Leisurely looks were cast in the direction of Candy who didn't seem to take any notice, possibly because she was so used to it.

They got away from the pandemonium of the ferry terminal – with its speeding taxis, people running, and crowded buses pulling in or leaving – and trudged along the packed pavement. There was little room for conversation until they turned into Canton Road. They walked the length of the ugly Y.M.C.A. building and turned the corner, walking round the huge bulk of the Peninsula Hotel.

"This is where we'll have lunch. I came here once with my father before the war, and it left a lasting impression on me. This is a day for re-living memories."

They reached the car park and Candy walked over to a magnificent Jaguar sports car. As she opened the door, she said:

"This was a birthday present from my husband. We've got a Cadillac for special occasions, but I like this better because it's my own."

He settled in the passenger seat, while she turned the ignition.

She backed out with ease and plunged into the deafening traffic along Nathan Road. Then she turned into Chatham Road and headed for the airport.

She drove self-confidently, accelerating in and out of the long lines of other vehicles. Relying on her driving skills, he began to take in every aspect of this jewel of a present.

Candy was busy complaining. Her house, its numerous servants, were one big headache. They would steal whatever they could, even though they were well paid. What had happened to the respectful servants of old? These people no longer showed any loyalty or friendship.

He listened to her with a sympathetic smile. How Candy must live well, up there on the Peak with all its luxuries, and with such a busy social life. Was she trying to impress him by boasting about her wealth and social status in Hong Kong? If this was her intention, then she was totally successful.

They came in sight of Kai Tak, under the roar of a plane taking off. Having parked the Jaguar, they penetrated the ground floor of the airport building amid voices in many tongues, and hundreds of people waiting to meet new arrivals. They went up to the first floor and saw more people crowded round the sales desks and check-ins of the different airlines, weighing cases and other luggage, talking in every language under the sun.

Near the gate leading to passport control, Candy found the people she was looking for. Some Englishwomen who greeted her in a warm and friendly way. He was introduced as a friend of long standing from Macau. One of the women had a child with curly blond hair and a nose full of freckles. He smiled at it, just as he did at all children. It made a face at him as if to tell him that he did not belong to its world.

He walked away. Then he remembered the day of his departure to Brazil. His parents had accompanied him as far as one of the wooden wharves that existed along the waterside boulevard. There was still a considerable amount of wreckage from the war – the scorched ruins of buildings behind, and in the waters, the twisted metal of sunken launches. His parents bit their lips, silent and tearful. Both promised to join him just as soon as they could. He would never see them again. Next to them stood his sister, whom he never imagined would emigrate to San Francisco some years later.

The English, unlike the Portuguese, never cry disconsolately when they say goodbye. Everything is done very discreetly, everybody is polite and reserved. Only the eyes are moist, but there is always some lighthearted comment to break the tension.

Judging by their clothes and by the quality of their shoes and handbags, they were not the social equals of Mrs Morris-White. But they were very close friends. When the monotonous voice announced that passengers for Canada should prepare for boarding, there were hurried kisses and recommendations. Then suddenly, they were alone.

"Well, there go two truly good friends. I shall miss them. I never like saying goodbye."

"Neither do I. It's always sad."

Candy didn't answer, but strode quickly towards the stairs, as if she were running away from the place. As he followed her, he thought to himself that in only a few hours he would be doing the same thing to this woman. He wondered how they would say goodbye to each other.

"Do you have anywhere in particular you want to visit?"

"No, I'm in your hands. You can take me wherever you like, just as long as we have lunch at the Peninsula."

The Jaguar once again ventured into the rumbling traffic, which absorbed the attention of both of them. Candy was as sure of herself as ever, smoothly and calmly changing gear, braking and accelerating. There's nothing like being next to someone who knows how to drive well. The car becomes an obedient animal, responding to the slightest touch of its master.

He sat back comfortably in order to enjoy the woman's skill.

After a few twists and turns, the Jaguar entered the Shatin area, heading in the direction of the hotel, which was situated on top of a hill. It was a pleasant, peaceful place, off the beaten track and ideal for a long conversation.

"Lets go and have an aperitif."

They sat on the terrace, with a magnificent view over the valley below them. The table was pleasantly shaded by a parasol. A waiter came over. He asked for a scotch and soda, Candy a dry martini.

Up until then, they had only swapped pleasantries. Now they would inevitably return to the past but words didn't come easily. After all, twenty-four years had gone by. They bided their time, admiring the landscape.

A train was returning from the border at Lowu, on its way to Kowloon. Puffing gently, it left a ragged trail of steam. On either side, there were rice paddies blotted with the dark shape of peasant workers at their daily toil. A river meandered, almost still. In the distance, a green stretch of sea, its waters flickering metallically in the light. An atmosphere of calm hung over the valley, so far from the bustle of the city they had left behind. For how long would it be spared the winds of progress and pollution?

Candy all but dominated the conversation. It was an entertaining monologue in which she described the boring games of bridge and canasta, the rounds of tea parties, the cocktails and receptions in the different consulates. Her talk still made an impression.

Then she started telling him about her children. She had three, the eldest was nineteen and studying electronic engineering in London. Her daughter was sixteen and causing her problems. She had a very close, exclusive circle of friends, and was growing away from her mother ever more quickly, while her role model was her father whom she adored. Her youngest son was the one closest to her.

> "I'm concerned about my daughter. I wish she were more modest, more unassuming. Far from it. She takes an exaggerated pride in her father's ancestry. That's why we don't get on. She's uppity, and we get on each other's nerves."

She stopped talking. There was a pause, while they sipped their drinks and smoked, gazing steadfastly at the view. Then Candy broke their silence to ask him about his life. Her questions masked an intense curiosity.

He answered simply. He had always thought of going abroad, because if you weren't a member of the liberal professions in Macau, there were no great openings for you. He had no great desire to join the civil service, with its poor rates of pay and its slow and frustrating climb up the hierarchy.

Straight after the war, a friend of his had written to him from Rio de Janeiro, painting a rosy picture of the country where there were opportunities for all those who wanted to work. It was hard overcoming his parents' reluctance. They were old and wanted their son near them, for their daughter sooner or later would get married and leave home. He answered their objections with eagerness. He promised to send for them, managed to engage their enthusiasm for the idea, and in the end they agreed. Their son was going to the land of milk and honey.

His first experiences of Rio were disheartening. If he hadn't invested so much money in going, he would have given up. Oh! The isolation of huge cities where no one knows anybody else, and people are selfish and taken up with their own problems. But then he got used to it and adapted. He had various jobs before joining the airline, where he now worked. He had begun as a mere clerical assistant, but with his good English he had got ahead fast, and now held an important post in the company. He had spent a few years in the United States, had been posted to Europe, and was in Portugal for a while. But now he was firmly based in Rio. He had a nice flat, and all the creature comforts.

"That's about it. I can't say I'm completely happy. Who is? Life takes as much as it gives. But I can't complain, at least in material terms."

He gulped his whiskey, while she leant forward, her chin cupped in her hands.

"Are you married?"

"I was."

"What about her?"

"She died in a stupid car accident two years ago."

"I'm sorry... What was she like?"

"She was a fun-loving girl, loved to talk, filled the house with her laughter and her singing. She was a Brazilian from

Porto Alegre. Much younger than me. I got to know her on a journey to New York. She was an airhostess. She spent all her free time on the flight talking to me. Six months later, we got married."

"Did you love her very much?"

"Yes, I think so. She was a very tender person and able to show it… But she's dead now."

"I'm sorry…"

"I've got used to the pain…"

"Do you have any children?"

"Two boys. They're staying with my parents-in-law, in fact they spend a lot of time with them. You understand, I lead a very busy professional life. The eldest is thirteen, the youngest ten. They want for nothing, except a mother."

"Do they look like you?"

"Like me and their mother. It's as if she lived on in them. That's one consolation."

A long silence descended on them, as they were both lost in their own thoughts. A young couple passed by, hand in hand, smiling, without seeing them, absorbed as they were in the pleasure of each other's company. When he turned to look at Candy again, he realized she had been gazing at him for some time. Now at last they were going to turn to their common memories.

"We could have been married."

"That's true… But it wasn't to be."

"It wasn't to be… The problem was the war. One couldn't take anything seriously."

"You're wrong. I got to the point when I took it very seriously."

"It was my fault. I didn't believe you. It started off as some fun, we had a great time. I wanted to put my poverty behind me. I didn't consider your feelings. I thought that when the time came for it, we would part without any ill feelings. But of course, there was never any commitment between us. You promised."

"Yes I promised. But promises are difficult to keep when the situation changes. I couldn't accept the idea of losing you after we had been so close."

They were talking about the past like two friends and as if they had nothing to do with the matter. The strangest thing was that they were able to refer to the most intimate details, as if there were no twenty-four year gap between them. Or maybe precisely because there was a gap.

"I wasn't a virgin."

"I knew what you'd gone through at the hands of the Japanese. By that time, it didn't make any difference to me."

"Don't tell me you didn't take me for a loose woman…"

"Maybe at first I did. But once I realized what a woman you were, I wanted to marry you."

"Then I must have been a huge disappointment to you."

He didn't want to say yes, because he needed to choose his words carefully in order not to offend her. No one likes to be accused of being a disappointment.

"Don't think about it. We might have made a mistake."

Candy opened her gold cigarette case and offered it to him. She lit their cigarettes with her lighter.

"Can you imagine what it would have been like if we had ended up together"

"Well, we would have had lots of children."

He said it jokingly, but then regretted it. Her look became pensive, sad. A solitary wrinkle cut across the smoothness of her forehead. She sighed and took another mouthful of dry martini.

At the time, she said, all she wanted was to find herself a rich man. She was young and sick of privation. She hadn't been born into a wealthy family, and had been orphaned when she was still little. She had been educated at Maryknolls because she had a generous godmother who had died of fright as a result of the war. During the bombing, she had seen her house destroyed and burned. He brother had been a volunteer and had died in combat. She'd been raped by three Japanese when she had foolishly gone out to look for bread the day after the surrender. She wasn't exaggerating the drama of it all. It had happened to a lot of girls in Hong Kong under the yoke of an invading force drunk with victory. It had been a nightmare… And what hunger she had experienced! When she got to Macau, all she wanted was to forget everything, have fun, and make the most of her youth.

She stubbed out her cigarette in the ashtray and went and leant on the iron balustrade, gazing into nothingness.

Do you remember? I had practically no clothes; I lived in a refugee centre where there was a lot of promiscuity. Once I had an attack of scabies. At the time there was a real epidemic of it. Do you remember? My hands and legs were covered in sores, I felt disgusted with myself. People would avoid me for fear of catching something. I hated being poor. I looked at myself in the mirror and saw that I was pretty. Why shouldn't I use my beauty to get ahead if it was the only thing of any value I had? So how could you expect me to take you seriously, you who were just a clerk in a commercial firm, waiting for the end of the war so that you could make a life for yourself?

"Yes, that was my worst fault: a clerk with a lousy income."

"I was impatient."

"You humiliated me."

"I'm sorry."

"It really doesn't matter anymore. I made some success of my life. And I didn't ask you to justify yourself."

"I'm not justifying myself. It all happened so long ago. But this is our chance to talk. I never wanted us to be bitter towards each other for the rest of our lives."

At a sign from them, the waiter brought some more drinks. They continued to sit in the shade, and the dry autumn breeze freshened their skin. A noisy group of Chinese students, boys and girls together, showed off their English and disturbed the peace of the terrace. But the interruption didn't affect them, settled as they were in a far corner.

He could no doubt remember Esteban, the Filipino she had gone around with. He was rich, or at least he had convinced her he was. He always had a wallet full of notes, he talked about his tobacco plantations in Mindanao, a gold prospecting concession in Baguio and other dazzling items of wealth. He had made her all the more eager when he talked about his house in the most exclusive area of Manila.

"Much later, I lived in one of those houses for a week. By that time I was married and my husband had gone to the Philippines on business. It was a wonderful week, and our hosts made us feel very welcome. But no one knew of Esteban or his family. All he had done was to describe what he had heard from others and what he had admired from a distance. But it isn't difficult to deceive an impecunious, naïve young girl. I was dazzled."

"Well, he caused an impression. He was handsome, cut a manly figure and no doubt had the air of someone who was wealthy."

"Yes, he had great seductive power, he was very generous and I just couldn't resist him. I was never hungry again… I dressed well, as well as one could during the war. I had to give him something in return…"

A sudden feeling of irritation welled up inside him. The resentment he thought had gone forever, rose to the surface again. It was, after all, just dormant.

"That's why you rejected me. He was better."

She drew back, shocked by the emotional tone of his voice. All those years were still insufficient for them to be able to examine things coldly. Gently and with humility, she said:

"You were both different. You had the inexperience of youth, you behaved like a romantic young boy. There was a delicacy in you that touched me deeply. It was good, really good."

"I don't understand."

"It's all very complicated. How can I explain? Esteban was an expert in the art of love making, he felt an almost pathological need to affirm his virility. I confused sensuality with love. I was very young too. At the time, I couldn't think things through, but I always felt in some way dirty. Today, I can see that our relationship could never have lasted. Degradation isn't a basis for lasting love… One gets tired, and sooner or later, shame will make its presence felt."

"But you dropped me for someone else."

"Yes, I did."

"You saw a better future in him."

"Looking at it coldly… yes. He was an ambitious soul."

They had almost finished their drinks. The group of students were making a lot of noise. The autumn breeze stirred the curls of Candy's abundant hair.

"Why are you looking at me like that? After getting your revenge a year later."

"Lets stop here."

"Tell me… That night at Repulse Bay was pure revenge… wasn't it?" After a moment's hesitation, he replied:

"Yes… I had to give vent to my humiliation."

"And did it make you happy?"

"At first, but then I felt ashamed. I didn't behave like a gentleman. Revenge left me with a bitter taste… You shouldn't have wept."

"Yes, I wept… because you were like Esteban in your violence. It was as if I didn't know you. You set out to humiliate me. Don't deny it, that's what you set out to do. You took advantage of a moment of weakness on my part. I was confused, adrift. Esteban hadn't written to me for two months. He'd left for Manila saying it would be a quick visit. But he never came back… I never heard from him again."

"I didn't know…"

"How could you? You were leaving for America. After getting your revenge, you weren't going to think of me again. I looked for you later… but you'd left Macau."

He could have told her he probably wouldn't have taken her back in such circumstances. But there was no point in hurting her just for the sake of it, and besides none of it mattered anymore.

"Then I moved to Canton where I muddled along working for foreign companies. When the communists came, I came back to Hong Kong."

"So everything turned out for the best. If you had married me, you wouldn't be what you are today, Mrs Morris-White of the Hong Kong social set, with a house on the Peak, a

Jaguar, a Cadillac... and goodness knows what else!"

She looked at him for a moment, as if she wanted to tell him something. Then she looked at her watch. It was time to return to the city if they wanted to have lunch at the Peninsula. By the time they paid their bill, they had apparently come to terms with the past.

They rushed back to Kowloon and left the Jaguar in the same car park where they had originally picked it up. They entered the hotel through the shopping arcade on the ground floor, reached the lounge and then went up to the first floor, walking over thick soft carpets. The Verandah Restaurant was full of diners, talking in the most diverse languages. They managed to get a table by the window, with a beautiful view over the harbour and the grey embankment that hugs the shore of the Island.

The headwaiter appeared, polished and efficient in his work. He knew Mrs Morris-White and was profuse in his friendliness. They ordered the lunch and a fine St Emilion to accompany the meat. They were distracted by the background murmur of conversation and the discrete tinkling of cutlery and china.

They were interrupted by an English couple, a husband and wife who showered them with polite consideration. They asked after Bill and reminded her of the trip to Cheang Chao Island on their yacht the following week. Candy introduced her companion as 'an old friend from Macau'. At that moment, she was the complete Englishwoman, with typical reserve, pauses in her speech and exclamations. The couple took their leave and were soon forgotten.

"You haven't taken your eyes off me. What's going on

inside your head?"

"You astonish me... Mrs Morris-White."

She shot him the mischievous smile he knew so well, and which made her look so young.

"Oh! Is that all? I make a lot of people astonished... and envious too."

"I'm not surprised people are envious. But tell me... just to satisfy my curiosity. How did you come to marry Morris-White? I'm told he's never out of the newspapers, he's a member of the grand Legislative Council, he's always travelling abroad promoting this territory's prodigious wealth."

Candy leant back in her chair with a languid look on her face. After taking a sip of St Emilion, she replied:

"It started with a couple of fried eggs and two slices of bacon."

His surprise amused her. That familiar mischievous smile hovered on her lips.

"Funny, isn't it? To anyone who asks, I paint a picture of a rosy romance, like Cinderella. After all, I might as well be allowed to tell a story about my meeting with Prince Charming. But the truth is that it all began with a couple of fried eggs and two rashers of bacon."

She had worked here and there in Canton. With the communist advance, she returned to Hong Kong, which was in the throes of massive development. New companies were opening up by the day, and offering work for all. She had become a first-rate typist, spoke excellent English, and was full of determination. She had a number of jobs before joining the huge firm where her future husband worked. She was one of dozens of workers in the typing pool. For months she passed unnoticed. She would see Bill, her future husband, coming and going from the various private offices, tall, upright, with a ruddy complexion, and with that distant air so common among Europeans once they pass Suez on their way to the East, bursting with arrogance, as if bearing on their shoulders the cross of the white man's burden. He didn't look at anybody, and ignored the minor functionaries as if they were merely part of the furniture.

> "We found it so annoying that he didn't even notice our existence. His haughtiness and superiority made us feel humiliated. Two or three times, I went into his grand office for small tasks. He would always utter a dry thank you, but he never even looked up or said anything else. This would have gone on forever, if something unforeseen and unusual hadn't occurred. You must understand that at the time, I never gave him a thought. Our superiors didn't socialize with us, they didn't belong to our rank, so that I never imagined that one day we might have a relationship."

She leant over the table to light a cigarette. She smoked and her hand remained in mid air, the lighter between her fingers.

> "As in all big cities, distances are huge here. To get to the office on time and not be fined, we'd often turn up without having had breakfast. We had to wait for coffee break before we could eat anything, unless we went to the bathroom to nibble some sandwiches. Now it so happened there was a room that wasn't being used and would make a perfect kitchenette. We put in a request, explaining our reasons. After some hesitation, the company eventually gave its consent. After that, we would make our coffee there, while

a boy made sandwiches and other snacks. I hate eating sandwiches in the morning. What I like is toast and eggs cooked in some way or other. In the fridge there were always eggs and bacon. I'm proud to say that I'm a dab hand at making fried eggs. You need a bit of skill to do them, even though it seems so easy, and I can say that I've got it."

The impish smile hovered on her lips as she recalled the past.

"One morning, I was starving when I arrived. I'd hardly had anything for dinner the previous evening and I spent the night dreaming of nice things to eat. I got there early and started to prepare my breakfast, and I really felt like eggs and bacon. I don't know whether it was I or someone else who left the door open. Bill had also come early. That day he hadn't had breakfast before leaving home. For some reason, he came down the corridor and got the full force of the smell of bacon and eggs. It must have been quite a sensation because he stopped short. I was carrying a plate when I surprised him. I was embarrassed, we said good morning in the usual way, and I asked him whether he would like some breakfast. He was a bit awkward, but when he saw my work of art, he gave in. Later I found out he adored fried eggs and bacon, like any good Englishman. He sat down and gobbled it all up, complementing me on my gifts as a cook. What's more, he drank two huge cups of coffee, asking me if I had made it. I lied, saying I had given the boy a hand. For the first time, he had noticed me. It was really humiliating that after this incident, I stopped being a piece of furniture and became a human being, all because of a dish of bacon and eggs."

He began to show an interest and found excuses to have breakfast with her. Bill must have sung the praises of her gifts to his colleagues. One by one they appeared, and although not something the organization encouraged, the separation between the hierarchies was partially broken. The kitchenette became a place where all staff were able to socialize. All this because of the miracle of bacon and eggs.

Some weeks later, Bill chose her to become his private secretary. Their relationship remained strictly professional, each one conscious of their position, he the boss and she the secretary, all prim and proper. Bill was Mr. Morris-White and she was Miss Candy.

> "As his secretary, I had to dress better. Was it my fault that my dresses fitted me well, showing off my contours and my taste? I can assure you that I didn't want anything from him at first. We lived in different worlds and although I was born in Hong Kong, my contact with English people had been superficial. They formed a close circle I didn't fit into. Bill was the first English person with whom I had any intimacy."

After a while, her woman's intuition made her realize that the distant Mr Morris-White was looking at her when he thought she was unaware. Ever more frequently, he had a nice word to say about her hair or her choice of dress. If they didn't leave the office together, they met in the street as if by coincidence. One day, he invited her for a drink.

> "So I became interested too. I was amused by the idea of seducing him. I planned ahead. If he thought his secretary was going to become his lover, which wasn't unusual, he was wrong. I played on my good looks, studied his habits and his tastes, and subtly wrapped my net around him so he couldn't escape. I went after him, with determination and using my wits. I played hard to get, I didn't sell myself cheap, and I refused to sleep with him."

Bill remained convinced that it was he who had seduced her. So as not to injure his male pride, she had allowed him to live with the illusion. The truth was that it was she who had seduced him. Bill began to rely increasingly on her company outside working hours, inviting her to dinner, to the cinema, to night clubs, moonlit trips round the Island in those little tourist ferries that can be seen crossing the harbour all lit up.

> "By this time, he was only Mr. Morris-White at work. I never slipped up. But when there were no strangers around, he was just Bill. I accepted his kisses and caresses, but I never went to bed with him. Bill was the soul of correctness, a real gentleman. I'm sure that at first he thought I would be an easy conquest, but what he found in me was a paragon of virtue. This played on his nerves. The more I gave him the slip, the more intent he became on conquering me. In the end he became jealous of my colleagues, and of his too. I watched him floundering in his efforts to maintain his British pretence at calm. My dear Bill! How I miss those days when I made you suffer so much!"

Eventually, he invited her to his home. It was a bachelor's flat, devoid of any woman's touch. As she thanked him, she promised to cook him an English dinner. She played the part of a housewife, introducing a homely feeling into his cold flat. Bill, dearest Bill, was conquered. He ate with renewed appetite, praised the quality of her dishes, and tucked into the food with gusto.

After dinner, they sat on the large sofa in the lounge. On the radio, they were playing the First Concerto for piano by Brahms. There was a growing intimacy between them, but just when Bill thought he was going to win his coveted prize, she politely but firmly refused. Bill got angry, sulked, but drove her home. He was a gentleman to the end. As they said goodbye, she told him that from then on their relationship should be restricted to matters of work. During the drive back, she had prepared what she was going to say, and spoke her words with the utmost serenity.

> "I was even afraid I had gone too far. It was a game… If I were to give in, I would be treated as a loose woman. It was win all or lose all. The following day, he treated me coldly. I behaved towards him as I always had, speaking to him naturally and with an assurance that I didn't feel deep down. We lived like this for a month. It was hard… it was awful! I realized the risk I was running. But it was vital not to weaken. I had to proceed firmly, without faltering, and with just one end in mind. I accepted invitations to dinner with colleagues of his, and Bill saw me once or twice dancing with his friends. I knew him well enough to be able to read his face. How jealous he was!"

One day, as she was preparing to leave after a particularly hard day's work, Bill summoned her to his office. There was nobody around to hear them, and Bill was pale and trembling, devoid of his usual sang-froid. Candy's heart began to beat faster and faster, as she sensed that her future was about to be decided.

"Will you marry me?"

"Are you serious?"

"I've never been more serious."

"Aren't you going to give me any time to think it over?"

"I need the answer now."

"Okay, I will."

"Tomorrow, we'll see to the paperwork."

"Fine."

"No more dinners or dances unless with me."

"I'm all yours."

"I can't live without you."

"Neither can I…"

"Then I don't understand."

"I want to be yours… but with a ring on my finger."

The company had never encouraged social relationships between management and the lower orders, and tried to put a stop to this marriage with a Eurasian, as she was considered. But Bill's decision was final. He was an excellent employee; they needed him and couldn't afford to lose him. Besides, by this time the British Empire was beginning to come apart.

There was another obstacle, and that was religion. Bill was a practising Anglican, and hated followers of the Pope. He insisted that his future wife should embrace his religion. At the time, his insistence didn't seem of great importance to her. She consented because she wanted to get married. At their wedding, the only guests were English people, and it was the same at the reception in the Hong Kong Club. Her family was conspicuous by its absence. In an attitude of defiance, they cut all contact with her.

"Bill gave me his name, and I repaid him generously. I picked up the rules of the game. I did my best to respond to the greatest challenge in my life. As Mrs Morris-White, I had many tasks to perform. I was accepted with some caution into my husband's world. I was always considered an outsider, deep down, a gold digger. I was watched, talked about, scrutinized. I put up with it all and never lost heart. I even found the challenge entertaining. I absorbed the habits of my husband and his people. I became English. It wasn't at all easy. You're probably thinking to yourself that I shouldn't have abandoned my roots. You're quite right. But it was a question of seeking happiness. If I wanted to accompany my husband and live in harmony with his social circle, I had to adapt. And what's true is that I did adapt. I tried to become a real English lady; I cultivated English taste, their expressions, gestures, even their food. My husband adored me. His secret fears remained unjustified. I had played my hand well and had won. I have nearly all I could wish for: my husband is faithful – at least, I'm not aware of any extra-marital affairs – and he indulges my desires."

But there followed a pause. A shadow passed over her eyes, as if she were suddenly assailed by some unexpected sadness.

They had finished their lunch. As someone who had come from Brazil, he found the steaming cup of coffee disgusting. Nevertheless, he sipped it slowly, as if he were fulfilling some ritual. She drank hers indifferently like someone exiled from the Latin taste for coffee. There was no doubt about it: she was the complete Englishwoman.

"From here you get a good view of the outline of the Island. Now guess where my house is."

He looked at the great bulk of the Peak with its houses and high-rise buildings dotted across its steep slopes. It was difficult. There were so many beautiful houses that it wasn't worth the effort. But to be nice, he took a guess and got it wrong. Then she pointed towards an elegant pink smudge set against the green mountainside. Seen from afar, it didn't reveal anything out of the ordinary. But its lofty position, with its magnificent view, were enough to guarantee that this was something truly exceptional.

> "My marriage was a success. Bill managed to get ahead, beat off his rivals in the organization, and achieve distinction. I helped him with heart and soul to rise to an important position. He was intelligent and competent, and I had boundless ambition. I helped him make courageous decisions which had positive results for him. I organized receptions, intimate tea parties, and dinners. I selected the guests, and made appropriate contacts. They were years of struggle, of planning, in which we were both united in a common end, and they were the best years of our life together. We had four children; one died. As you can see, I managed to achieve something in life."
>
> "You can't complain. You have no right to. Otherwise you might tempt fate."

She paused again. The food and wine made them feel somewhat languid and drowsy. Candy was no longer so exuberant, as if telling her life's story had drained her of all enthusiasm.

> "None of my children takes after me. They are all blond and very English. Even the one who died. There's no trace of anything oriental in them. My husband's blood is really quite extraordinary. On occasion, people have even asked me whether they are my stepchildren. They couldn't believe that I was their mother. Bill gets angry about it. But it was as if my womb had played the worst possible trick on me."
>
> "But at least you have something I don't have. A daughter.

I'm good friends with my boys, but they're offhand. They don't keep me company. A daughter would fill my house with love and make it seem less empty."

Candy's eyes suddenly filled with tears, and she reached across the table to take his hand. He was touched by her gesture and was unable to continue.

She recomposed herself and took out her compact, while he asked for the bill. Not long afterwards they got up, she walking elegantly ahead, he behind her, proud of her being with him. And she could have been his wife…

They went down to the bustle of the ground floor. In the lounge, the tables were still full. At the reception, there was a group of Americans talking loudly in their nasal accent, as if the world belonged to them. They walked along the arcade full of shops, where the gravity of the assistants gave it an English air. Candy went into a boutique, asked to see the ties and made her choice with great care. It was a Pierre Cardin design, blue with red dots. She paid and gave it to him.

"It's a souvenir. Every time you wear it, you'll think of me."

Once in the street, they made for the Jaguar. The pavement was nearly empty except for a stunningly beautiful girl approaching them, her hair floating in the autumn breeze. She was wearing a tight cheongsam, with its traditional slit on the sides and its high collar. She didn't look totally Chinese, but more like a Macanese. As he watched her somewhat audaciously, he was reminded of Candy during the war years. The girl passed by without noticing them, her attention concentrated on something up ahead. Candy didn't even notice her, as she opened her bag to get her car keys.

"Did you see the girl who passed by just now?"

"Who?" she asked, distractedly.

"The one over there. Do you know who she reminded me of? You. She's the image of you in the old days."

Candy turned hurriedly to look back, and caught sight of the girl as she bent down to get into a large Chevrolet. Candy's expression had changed. He realized he had made a mistake. A woman should never be reminded of her youth, nor should comparisons be made to her face! In trying to be nice, he had gone too far and been hugely stupid.

Once in the car, Candy seemed lost in her own thoughts. The car shot off at an unnecessary speed. He heard a cry of protest from a pedestrian behind them. She carelessly overtook a taxi that had to brake hard.

"So, she looked like me… Her face was like mine back in the days of the war."

"Well, don't take it literally. She just reminded me of you. It was all so quick, just a fleeting impression. You were better, just as you still are… more beautiful."

That made things worse. He felt truly unhappy for not having chosen his words better.

"How old was she?"

"I've no idea… maybe twenty something."

"That wasn't quite what I meant."

He was dumbfounded. Candy didn't seem to hear him, her eyes apparently intent on the street full of traffic.

The Jaguar headed for the Yaumati terminal, for the car ferry over to the Island. They joined the queue and waited for their turn, while Candy complained about the delay. When the new tunnel was open, they wouldn't waste so much time.

The car glided down the gangway, and drew up deep inside the ferry. They were now sandwiched between trucks. When the vessel began to move, they got out of the Jaguar and went and stood at the bows.

The green waters reflected flickeringly the particles of golden sunlight. A passenger liner sounded its siren, signalling departure. A little further out, an oil tanker slid towards its buoy.

Her mood had dispersed, but there was a dark shadow of melancholy in her eyes. It wasn't the joyous Candy of earlier in the day.

> "My husband is away, visiting Lantao, and only gets back this evening. You won't have a chance to meet him. He's completely absorbed in his work. There are always meetings, interviews, quite apart from his office hours. And what a busy social life we lead! Cocktails, dinners, lunches, bridge sessions, visits to social assistance projects, inaugurations, receptions, balls, parties organized by the sports association and the church! Just as we think we are about to get some free time, which isn't often, along come some people to disturb a peaceful evening. We hardly have any family life nowadays. Our children are growing up, and we don't have a chance to be with them. My husband thrives on this way of life. He never gets tired, he's got an iron constitution. The heroic days are over. My husband no longer needs me, nor does he even ask my advice. We've reached the top. With or without me, he'll win. Next New Year he'll get a knighthood and I'll be Lady Candy."

The smell of the sea mixed with that of gasoline. There were patches of oil and rubbish on the water's green surface. The Island grew before their eyes, its buildings gleaming in the afternoon sun.

"Some years ago, the distinction would have filled me with fear. Now I can accept it without celebration. Do you know I've reached saturation point? I've begun to miss my old world, my own people. I keep remembering my childhood and adolescence. Back then, I had such lust for life, I had so many friends. We were always having parties, dances, picnics. All that vanished. My friends of old don't speak to me, my relatives have turned away... As far as they are concerned, I'm English, something from another world."

She lit a cigarette, and inhaled desperately. She gazed at the view, but without taking it in.

"It was my fault. I devoted myself entirely to my husband, to his career and ambition. I lost contact with my own folk, I even looked down on them. I didn't mind offending sensitivities, and I caused a lot of resentment. They never forgave me for agreeing to an Anglican wedding and to bringing my children up as Anglicans. They don't consider me to be married. Many years ago, I got an anonymous letter calling me a 'golden whore'. I should have acted differently... Now, it's too late to go back... I should never have cut the link with my family, my ancestral roots."

She let out a bitter little laugh as she lit another cigarette, after having stubbed the first one out only half smoked. This was a Candy full of anguish, burdened by a secret unhappiness.

As the ferry was getting near to the Island, they returned to the Jaguar. Candy turned on the radio and for some minutes they sat listening to dance music.

> "What a pity you have to leave so soon… I've still got so much to tell you… It's my confession. I have everything a woman from a poor background could aspire to. But I feel an emptiness around me. The Faith I was brought up in is a matter of concern to me and I say the prayers I learnt as a child. It's ridiculous, after twenty-one years of marriage, for me to be saying these things."

What could he say by way of an answer? Console her, insist that she was still beautiful, attractive, a woman still capable of loving and being loved? Did she deserve pity?

> "My husband knows nothing about you or about Esteban. The only thing he knows is that I was raped by the Japanese. During our heroic years, when we were building up our life together, he couldn't stand them. Now, he often goes to Japan and has lots of Japanese friends. It no longer seems to matter to him."

The ferry was now docking, and they could hear all the car engines starting up. With her hands gripping the steering wheel, Candy burst out:

> "In a few years, I'll be fifty. Am I to shrivel up and die, without a child who looks like me?"

They drove up the gangway onto the Island, and edged in among the noisy traffic on Connaught Road. For a split second she lost control of the car and it almost ran into a truck. He shivered with fright, but Candy didn't even hear the oath shouted by the other driver, more scared than angry.

> "I'm a sinful woman…"

They left the built up area of Victoria and began to climb the hill. Judging by the direction they were going, he realized she was driving towards Repulse Bay. He didn't say a word, but busied himself by taking in the changes the Island had gone through during all the years he had been away. On every side, new buildings rose skywards, swallowing up the peaceful, verdant areas of old. All so different from Hong Kong at the end of the war, with the scars of a city reborn from the rubble and poverty, with great piles of rubbish scattered around here and there.

Repulse Bay came into view round a bend in the road, its beach of white sand open to the sun, its calm waters caressing the shore with a fringe of foam. The vegetation on the slopes above it was as abundant as ever and new residences dotted the hillside with white and yellow.

They parked the Jaguar in a shady spot and walked up to the hotel, which still preserved its colonial character, with its wide porch and balconies, evocative of the past and the Empire. Inside, people conversed in hushed tones, in an atmosphere that was quintessentially English. There were no vestiges to remind them of the war.

They strolled through the garden and went down to the beach along winding paths. It thoroughly merited its name. It gave off a restful, even idyllic air. The afternoon, now in decline, radiated all the crystalline purity of the autumn.

Side by side, neither of them mentioned the night they had been there, twenty-four years before. There was no need, for their silence spoke more eloquently than any words.

He had come over to Hong Kong to see to the final preparations for his journey to Brazil. It had been an emotional moment when he received the ticket that would get him to the other side of the world. He was due to leave in ten days' time. When he got in touch with a friend, he accepted an invitation to his birthday party, without mentioning to him that he was about to go away. He would leave his farewells to the last possible moment.

On his way to the party, he had a premonition that he would run into Candy. Maybe that was the main reason for his not turning down the invitation. His friend was a former refugee he had got to know at the same time as the girl. And he wasn't mistaken.

When he arrived, the party had already begun. The recent effect of war was still visible in the clothes people were wearing and in the simplicity of the food. But everyone was unusually merry, and this reflected the absence of inhibitions and tension. The euphoria of the immediate post-war period was still there.

He didn't see Candy for the first hour. In the lounge, a tiny orchestra of amateur musicians played Glenn Miller, Harry James and Xavier Cugat, all very much in fashion at the time. People danced the jitterbug frenetically, followed by rumbas and then sad and sentimental slows. The traditional hospitality of the Hong Kong Portuguese had not lessened in the slightest. There was laughter, flirtation, jokes, and there were plenty of girls to dance with or talk to.

He had forgotten all about her when, suddenly he heard her familiar peal of laughter. Whether nearby or far away, that laugh of hers was unmistakable. He felt a rush of blood to his face and ears.

She was standing by a table surrounded by a group of boys. He didn't know when she had arrived. She was wearing a tight brown dress to die for, which matched the tone of her skin and colour of her hair. Her face was too heavily made up, and her lipstick made her look tremendously sensual.

This wasn't the Candy of wartime, but a beautiful, seasoned Candy, who looked quite simply well off. He was overcome by bitterness, amazed at his own jealousy. This was Esteban's work and he wasn't there. The girl talked and chatted, apparently unaware of his presence.

At that moment, a boy jumped up behind the drums and put on a loud show in imitation of Gene Kupra. Everybody's attention turned towards the performer, and Candy's more than anyone else. When he finished, she stepped forward and gave him a congratulatory kiss. Then, she turned round.

They saw and greeted one another, she with the most natural of smiles, and he because he would have felt isolated if he had uttered some offensive comment. They didn't exchange a word, and Candy was led off by someone to dance a swing.

Taking a large gulp of whiskey, he pondered. What was the point of sulking and being resentful, if in ten days' time all this would no longer matter as wider horizons opened up for him? There was something absurd about his rancour, and displays of hurt pride wouldn't make the girl more or less interested in him.

The moment he heard the first strains of *Moonlight Serenade*, he didn't hesitate. He burst onto the dance floor and went up to Candy, cutting in front of another boy. They danced. He made every effort not to show how nervous he was. The perfume of her bath soap hovered over her, and he found this disturbing. They talked. There was no mention of the past, as if they were no more than acquaintances. He lied that he was working in a government department, she said candidly:

"I'm engaged. I'm getting married in a couple of months."

If that was a hint for them to forget their resentment, he didn't respond to it. He made no comment. The band played other tunes, and he stood back as other boys came to ask her for a dance. Back at the bar, with another drink in his hand, he chewed over his bitter feelings towards Esteban, the Filipino who had stolen her from him. The humiliation he had suffered was still alive. He felt a need for revenge in order that his rival should not be able to laugh at him forever and a day.

He danced with her again, and they were together when the last number was played. As they said goodbye to their host, Candy asked:

"Are you okay for transport?"

"No… I'll catch a taxi on the corner."

"Then come with me. I've got room in my car."

He thanked her and they walked down together. They got into the car, a pre-war Ford, but still in good condition, accompanied by a friend who had come with Candy. They didn't take more than a quarter of an hour to deliver the girl home, and when they were alone, she asked:

"Are you tired?"

"No."

"We can go for a drive. I don't feel like sleeping."

It was something of an invitation. The car glided swiftly along, while she talked about her job, about life in Hong Kong which, although suffering the devastating effects of war, was recovering rapidly. She displayed a pride in her city and confidence in the future, which contrasted with her doubts of old, those of a refugee who had lost everything.

He barely listened to her, possessed with a growing excitement that caused his blood to boil. He only had one thing in mind: to get his revenge and make a cuckold of Esteban. To put it bluntly, that was what he wanted.

They passed through Pokfulan and arrived at Repulse Bay, where they pulled up in the car park by the beach. At that hour the place was deserted. Night hid the vestiges of war, the hillside was bathed in darkness. There were lights in the hotel although he didn't know whether it was functioning as one or not.

She switched off the engine and got out of the car. He followed suite and they walked towards the beach. It was clear she wanted to talk, but he didn't give her time. He pulled her towards him and kissed her full lips impetuously. Candy tried to protest with an indignant cry, but this only provoked him more.

"No… no…"

Now he realized it wasn't just to make the other man a cuckold. It was more than that. He wanted to make love to her, to ravish her, to seize control of her and so satisfy his furious craving for possession. They rolled around on the sand and her resistance gradually died down. She seemed to want him too. He penetrated her deeply with bull-like force, releasing all his pent up humiliation and frustration in one long orgasm. As he withdrew from her, his first thought was for Esteban. Wherever he was at that moment, he hoped he had a heavy head.

She began to weep quietly. In his triumph, he failed to console her. He wanted to enjoy his victory and her tears were therefore irrelevant.

"Don't cry! What's done is done."

They didn't exchange another word. They drove off, the girl weeping as she gripped the wheel. The Ford zigzagged its way up the road. His sense of triumph gradually left him to be replaced by a feeling of shame. After all, he had raped the girl, taken advantage of her weakness and treated her like some cheap whore.

"Stop the car. I'll get out here…"

Candy obeyed, and he got out of the car without another word and walked off. The noise of the car grew fainter as it was swallowed up by the night, and he made no attempt to call her back.

The following morning he went back to Macau and ten days later he returned to Hong Kong, but only for a few hours prior to boarding his ship for Brazil. He didn't see Candy again for twenty-four years, but he never forgot the low sound of her weeping…

Candy must also have been remembering that night, sitting there beside him, for suddenly she said:

"It was all so painful… so unexpected."

"Yes… I didn't behave like a gentleman."

"Don't blame yourself. It was partly my fault too. I shouldn't have brought you here at such an hour. If I had been more determined in resisting you, we wouldn't have gone so far. But I was so alone. Esteban hadn't written to me for two months and I was terribly frightened that he had left me. When I danced with you, I realized that if we'd gone on being lovers I wouldn't have felt such fear. I brought you here because I wanted to talk to you, to tell you the truth about my life. You didn't give me time. All you wanted was revenge."

"It was a moment of madness, but I had suffered a lot too."

"That night could have been decisive for both of us, if you hadn't left. It might have been a chance for us to get back together again. How everything would have turned out differently."

"Yes, but for you, things turned out better anyway."

They were now on their way to the Peak, for Candy had insisted on showing him her fabulous house. The landscape was magnificent, with views over the harbour, the hills of Kowloon and, much further away, their outline made hazy by the distance, the mountains of China.

After a while, the Jaguar turned off the road and began to climb a steep driveway. At the entrance, a sign arrogantly proclaimed the word 'Private'. On either side grew rows of acacias and forest-oak, producing a welcome, rustling shade. There was a comforting twitter of birds settling down for the night.

At the top of the drive, an iron gate opened automatically as the car approached. The house came into sight in the background, painted all in pink, with a wide veranda which exhibited both comfort and opulence. The colonial windows, with their green shutters in the traditional style, stood out against the pink walls. There was a tennis court, a swimming pool with blue waters, lawns and flowerbeds containing seasonal blooms, exuberant in the dying heat of the sun.

In the garage, apart from the Cadillac, there was another car. It was a Sunbeam-Talbot belonging to the eldest son, who used it when he came home on holiday.

When the Jaguar pulled up by the front door, the family's chauffeur appeared immediately. The houseboy in his crisp white tunic also came to the door.

They passed through the hall and went into the vast sitting room, which was furnished in the modern style, with sofas and armchairs to satisfy the most exigent of tastes. The harmony and balance of some refined interior designer reigned supreme there. A huge grand piano took pride of place among the furnishings, giving an air of nobility, but without detracting from the overall ambience of the room. On the walls, apart from a picture of the Queen, there were paintings evoking the Empire and Old Hong Kong.

He sat back in one of the sofas admiring the plushness of it all, and refused a cigarette in order not to soil the crystal ashtray. Two doors opened onto the garden, peaceful in the metallic light of the dying sun. A gardener moved about with a hose from where a last jet of water glistened.

Candy then showed him the dining room with its long, lustrous table for twelve people, in very dark, well polished wood, amid the glint of glass from the cupboards and chandeliers. After that, they went to the husband's study, a games room for billiards, poker and bridge, with a bar at the back, the children's play room, the huge kitchen and the pantry, in a corner of which the family took their breakfast. All the rooms contained the necessary refinements for the function they served.

They didn't go upstairs where, according to Candy, there were only bedrooms.

He abstained from what might have been seen as an invasion of privacy. Certainly, it was a house of one's dreams, fully deserving of all the praise it received.

> "Well, you've seen where I live. Lets go to Bill's study. There are some books there to keep you entertained. I need to make some phone calls. I've been away from my usual life for a few hours, and now I need to catch up on a few things..."

He agreed. Outside, the half-light of autumn predominated. He glanced at his watch. In an hour's time, he would be leaving this mansion. He felt unaccountably touched. The boy brought him a whiskey and soda and one or two things to pick at. For the lady, there was a dry martini.

He examined the picture of a smiling Bill, the perfect man in his early fifties, in the pose of an empire builder. He was the complete Anglo-Saxon, tall and well built. He had a determined mouth, and the arrogant eyes of someone used to victory. What a contrast with Candy's dark, oriental Portuguese face!

The books had a pleasant smell about them and didn't seem to have been greatly used. There were a lot of technical works on administration and the economy, the management of banks and firms. Some novels, many volumes on political matters, collections of British classics and beautifully bound books on art. In addition, there were some travel books, which had no doubt been ordered for decoration rather than for educational purposes.

Candy was on the telephone. She had once again become the perfect Englishwoman, with a diction that never ceased to surprise him. For about a quarter of an hour, he overheard her arranging her social commitments, which she carried out scrupulously. One of the calls concerned an order to a supplier for a certain Bordeaux wine she wanted for a dinner party the following Monday. In another call, she was the amiable, fascinating woman, organizing a game of bridge. Then, she phoned to apologize for not being able to attend a certain reception because of a prior commitment. After that, there was a call to wish someone a speedy recovery and a promise to visit. Then there were other calls where she sought to keep the conversation to a minimum.

> "I've finished at last! I'm sick of it. Everyday, it's the same thing… It's a stupid life where you have to keep a permanent smile on your face. When will I ever be free of it?"

She swallowed her dry martini in one go, and refilled her glass.

> "Recently, I've been drinking too much."

When she noticed he was eyeing his watch again, she became agitated. Her ladylike composure began to dissolve.

> "This is a dream house… so people say, but it's not a home. We scarcely make use of it. If we're not out at some social function we have people here to spoil our afternoon or evening, social impositions rather than visits from friends. Oh! If only you didn't have to go so soon…"

> "I've got to go back because of my work. It's the call of duty for me too…"

> "I won't be able to introduce you to Bill."

> "I'll feel I know him having seen his photo here."

No, he certainly didn't want to meet him. What would be the point? Bill might even find it strange. He was a man from Candy's past, whom she had buried long ago. What was most likely was that he would never again see this woman, who drowned her immense sorrow in drink, sitting there in her gilded cage. Where, then, was one to find happiness?

At that point, a teenage girl appeared, rosy skin and English features, the image of the man in the photo. This was Evelyn. Physically, she and her mother had nothing in common.

She displayed the usual social graces when Candy introduced her. But she kept her distance, with that haughty air of formality that the English have when they don't want to exchange any familiarities. She looked at their drinks with a reproachful air, as if the two of them were violating some sanctuary.

"You're sitting in my father's favourite chair."

Before either of them could reply, a little boy, nine years old at the most, came in. This was Tom, fairer and even more English looking than the sister, his nose full of freckles. He addressed the guest very formally and confidently as 'sir'.

For those two siblings who stood there watching him, without any obvious hostility, but at the same time without any interest, he realized that he was surplus to requirements. Apart from this, the mother was no longer Candy, but Mrs Morris-White and the punctilious English with which the three addressed each other further increased the sudden chill in the room.

He waited for the children to move away and got up.

"I've got to go, Candy."

"I'm sorry about the children. They always behave like that with strangers. I can't seem to get them to change."

"It's natural. They're not used to finding someone like me

in this house. I don't belong to their world."

Candy had another dry martini. They remained silent for a while, until he lit a cigarette. By now he no longer cared about dirtying the ashtrays.

"Let me have your card. Maybe one day I'll turn up in Brazil."

He gave her one. Candy was once again stricken with anxiety. It was time to go.

"I'll walk to the end of the drive and take a taxi."

"I won't hear of it. A-Veng will take you in the car."

Before he could protest, she left the study, walking steadily. He finished his whiskey and put out his cigarette. He stared vacantly at the triumphant face in the photo.

Candy returned. Outside, the last rays of daylight filled the windowpanes with flashes of gold.

"Goodbye Candy… Thank you for a lovely day."

"The pleasure was mine… You're sure you don't resent me anymore?"

"No. I just feel very happy for having spent the day with you."

He held out his hand and she came over and took it. They looked at each other and then, suddenly, fell into each other's arms and kissed. When they separated, there were tears in Candy's eyes. She wouldn't let go of his hands, and her lips were trembling as she tried to speak.

"I gained all this… a place in the sun. I have everything a happy woman would want. But I should have married you."

"Don't say that."

"Yes, it would have been a different type of life, but I wouldn't have felt so alone, abandoned by my people, deprived of my true faith. Do you know why these children don't look like me? And do you know why you don't have a daughter? It's a punishment…"

She bit her lips to try and control a sudden burst of anguish and continued:

"It's about time someone shared my secret. That night at Repulse Bay, you made me pregnant. I went to Macau to look for you when I discovered what had happened, but you'd left. I tried to get an abortion but I didn't have the courage. To hide my shame I went to Canton. I went through hell there. Then the baby was born, and it was a nightmare. It was a girl. In a moment of despair, and because I couldn't justify her, I gave her away to a Chinese couple who didn't have any children. The little child looked like me, she was the picture of us both, and I gave her away to strangers. They disappeared without trace. When I felt the first surge of remorse, I searched, I tried to find her, but it was too late. I lost my daughter… our daughter."

She spoke in a whisper. She continued to hold his hands, as if contact would save her.

"I was shocked when you mentioned the girl who looked like me. Who knows whether it wasn't our lost daughter? How many times might we have passed each other, how many times might we have stood side by side? Oh, I'll never…"

"Candy."

"If I'd married you, I would never have felt this remorse that seems to get worse the older I grow. Our children would be ours, with our face, and they would share their parents' faith and I would never have had… a daughter out there, lost. That's why I was never able to forget you."

The sound of Tom playing in the garden brought her down to earth. She wiped away her tears and controlled herself as she whispered to him:

"Go now… I'm sorry I told you all this, but you had to know. Vengeance isn't always the pleasure of the gods. I'm a sinner. Go… A-Veng is waiting for you."

He walked away in a daze, without looking back. Dusk was now no more than a deep red stain. High above, the first stars twinkled. The chauffeur stood stiffly as he opened the door of the Cadillac for him, and so he bade farewell to that house of dreams…

MARIA ONDINA BRAGA

Born in Braga, Portugal, in 1932, she lived in England and France, before becoming a teacher in Angola, Goa and Macau between 1959 and 1965. In 1982, she was invited to teach Portuguese at Beijing University. She is a translator and the author of a considerable body of fiction, as well as collections of essays and travel writing. Some of her work bears the influence of her experiences in the Far East – most notably, *A China Fica ao Lado* (1968), *Angústia em Pequim* (1984), and her prize winning novel, *Nocturno em Macau* (1991). Her fictionalised autobiography, *Estátua de Sal* (1963), was written during her four-year stay in Macau.

THE MAD WOMAN

It was during the summer holiday at Cheok-Vân beach, on the island of Coloane.

She would come and sit on the boulders by the water, after sunset. We never saw her arrive. She would appear suddenly on the rocks, silently, like a lizard.

Thin, with her greying braid, her smooth, sad face cupped in her hands, she would fix her gaze upon some distant point, never returning our good afternoons, never moving, unaware of anything.

No one knew where she lived or whether she had a family. The Chinese even avoided looking at her.

In the wooden bungalow, I would wake up in the middle of the night, thinking of her: was she mad? Would she still be sitting there, gazing into the darkness, her feet in the water, her face in her hands?

Sam-Lei, the maid, had told me a story about her that was doing the rounds:

The mad woman had fled from Mainland China with her baby, who had died in exile. Her husband, who was supposed to follow her, never arrived. Having buried her child at the beach, she would come and wait for her husband at nightfall. She herself had fled by night. It was at night too that the husband would escape. At night the dead came back to life. And every night, the mad woman would sit there waiting...

At the big house on the hill – the palace of A-Tim - the peacock would shriek in the early morning, and Sam-Lei, the old maid, believed it was the mad woman in the agony of daybreak.

The mad woman didn't like the sun. No one ever caught sight of her during the day. Only at night would she emerge, with her tattered coat, her dirty grey braid, her bare feet, and her face lost in thought.

I even got up very early to see if I could find her, although I never did so before sunrise.

It was the time of day when the giant snails swarmed over the island's paths. Huge, red, rubbery things, they would drag themselves in a beeline towards the patches of yam, or the climbing plants along the walls, their heads raised and feelers erect. Boats would be setting out for the fishing grounds. The mad woman's rock would sometimes disappear under the waves that lapped against the stilts of the porch in front of the temple. There was no sign of the woman. And I, ever fearful that the sea had taken her away, would anxiously wait for nightfall.

But at dusk, there she was again, immobile, looking into the distance.

The maid would laugh at me.

"She can't die because she's already truly dead. She's a divided spirit. A shadow. Nothing can happen to her anymore, whether good or bad. She's dithering between life and death. She's nothing."

Did I think the mad woman's body had any consistency? I should touch her and I'd see for myself. (Certainly, no one had ever touched her. Her braid, tied together with wispy *ficus* roots, was sprinkled with ash from the temple, and her feet were glass fishes.) Had I never noticed the mad woman's feet? Long, flat, transparent, they floated on the surface of the water like dead fish.

One day, Sam-Lei had heard her laugh, and her laughter was like a gust of wind in the depths of a cave. She had no insides. She had no soul. She was hollow.

I asked:

"And what about the screams in the early morning?"

"That's the hour when she reencounters her wandering spirit. That's when she knows her husband won't come and that her child doesn't belong to her anymore. Her scream is one of pain, realization, defeat. But it all happens in a split second. Then, off she goes again, once more nobody."

"It's the peacock, you know that only too well."

"Peacocks only shriek at night, when they sense a tiger nearby. There are no tigers in Coloane. It's not the peacock."

And every night, there was the mad woman on the beach, her feet in the water, head in hands. And no one ever saw her arrive.

When children passed by, they would whisper:

"She smells of another world, for sure…"

The mad woman neither moved, nor heard, nor saw.

Sam-Lei advised me not to go near. It was dangerous.

"By day, she lives in a hole in a tree… an owl! Maybe even another bird, or a bat. By night, she takes the shape of a person, and goes to await her ghosts."

It was round about that time that my friend, Mei-Lai, came to Coloane, and the two of us decided to solve the mystery of the mad woman.

We wouldn't go to bed; we would stay on the beach, sitting on the rocks all night, if necessary. When she eventually went home (she must after all have a home), we would follow her.

It was a very sultry night, and so it was almost a pleasure to be outdoors. Mei-Lai carried a torch, which we would only light if it really became necessary, so as not to scare the woman, and a little bag of peanuts to pass the time.

We chatted for hours on end in hushed tones.

Time went rushing by. One, two, three hours. The moon was up, a full, clear moon that tore a pearl-strewn path through the sea. The waves tirelessly repeated their all-embracing litany.

I remembered that such nights in Africa filled the locals with terror, because it was then that the animals (half god, half devil) chose to mate – crocodiles would make love and snakes would nestle in the warm sands of the beach. Such clear nights would induce anguished dreams, and the black woman, Águeda, would utter a prayer to "the nightmare of holed hands and scarlet fingernails". We would die by suffocation if the nightmare's hands didn't have holes in them, the hands he used to cover our mouths.

Mei-Lai told me about the superstitions of her country. On moonlit nights, her grandmother would put a sandstone plate full of poppy seeds out on the porch, to protect the house from wandering spirits. The poppy, with its hypnotic poison, made them drowsy. In the morning, she knew they had passed by because of a light cloud of smoke – so light that Mei-Lai could never make it out – drifting away from the plate.

A warm breeze blew off the sea.

We fell silent.

Then, the murmuring of the waves, along with the hushed whisperings of the beach, suddenly ceased.

It was as if Nature were respectfully preparing itself for some solemn spectacle, maybe the struggle between night and day, maybe the mad woman's agony.

My Chinese friend drew closer to me. We hardly dared utter a word. We hardly dared look in the direction of the woman with the dirty grey braid. We hardly dared move.

> "I've never felt so scared in all my life. What's going to happen?"

And the peanuts spilled from our hands, rolling over the stones like drops of water.

We looked at each other in surprise. Then, as if of one and the same mind, our eyes sought out the mad woman. Sure enough, there she was huddled on her rock, water round her ankles, inert, ghostlike.

It must have been about four o'clock. Suddenly, the peacock let off its shriek.

The cry came from the direction of the house of A-Tim, the rich man, further up the beach. It was his peacock. I almost laughed. Mei-Lai sighed.

> "We'll tell Sam-Lei it was the peacock after all," my friend decided. And her voice, though hushed in tone, echoed in a singular fashion.

By now the moon was very high, while a vague light seemed to be emerging from somewhere, whether the mountain or the sea, we couldn't be sure.

The things around us seemed deformed. A tuft of cacti over there looked like an open hand, huge and aggressive. The rocks were wild animals, beasts: reclining lions, bears rearing up on their hind legs, buffaloes ready to charge you. The jade rings on Mei-Lai's fingers had grown pale, like the eyes of a cat.

But what about the mad woman? We stared at the place. The tide was still low. The rock was there. She, however, had vanished.

> "But I only saw her a minute ago!" we both said at the same time.

We ran along the beach. Not a living soul. We glanced at the sea, deserted, impassive. As morning approached, the water was turning a reddish colour, and the sand, white only moments before, had darkened, just as if instead of Cheok-Vân, we were at Hak-Ça – Black-Sand.

We walked slowly back to the bungalow, in silence.

At the kitchen door, Sam-Lei was waiting for us.

> "It was the peacock that cried, we're sure!" But only our voices showed any conviction.
> "And so, what about her?" asked Sam-Lei, without obtaining a reply. "Ah! I spent the whole night clutching this charm so that nothing bad would happen to you! It's dangerous to take risks like that…"

And she gave each of us a dish of tea. I can still taste the bitterness of that beverage in my mouth. It tasted strongly of star anis. Perhaps it was some filter against the evil eye.

THE LEPERS

When the sun sank into the sea, the hill at the end of the island was a flaming torch. It was as if the world were going to end there, or perhaps begin, as if new forms, or else nothingness, were about to emerge decisively from the fiery mass of elements – clayish earth, sky and water set alight by the breath of the Spirit – and as if whatever time span were to begin there, it would do so with a perfect day in which nature had been cleansed.

A-Mou, whose face was marked by one or two of the red spots of a leper, went out every day to admire the sunset, trembling with anxiety and hope.

It was the hour when the other patients would retire to the corner of their bunks, either because the reflection of the sun in the sea burned their infected eyes, or merely because of some secret, inexplicable superstition.

A-Mou was young, and the disease, still in its initial stage, caused her no suffering. Indeed, all she had were the spots. The doctor had promised to cure her. She loved life, she liked to beautify herself with coloured dresses, flowers in her hair, varnish on her nails.

Late afternoon, hugging her beloved guinea pig, which slept at the foot of her bed like a cat, A-Mou would climb to the top of the hill, dreaming of a new, different, and better tomorrow.

One could see the whole island from up there: the marshy rice paddies down in the valleys, glimmering in the last rays of sunshine; the plantations of tea and of yam in terraces along the steep slopes; the black and yellow stones among the evergreen clumps of fir trees. And to gaze upon the island was, in some way, like contemplating the world, catching a glimpse of life beyond the leper colony. In the wide curve of sea, boats returned from the fishing grounds. Then, night descended upon the Earth. And A-Mou's romantic soul was filled with faith, with a feeling of warmth towards existence itself, with a happiness that brought tears to her eyes.

The others thought her strange: while they, like proper Chinese, enjoyed company, gossip, noise, especially as night fell, A-Mou liked to be alone. She didn't behave like a Chinese, they remarked. And if they asked her why she went out alone at that hour, she just smiled. She wouldn't say, nor would she know how to say it, that it was just because no one else went out, because something supernatural marked the moment, because it was dark when she returned, the first toads, the first field mice would venture out onto the path – and she would wait for them to start talking, just like in childhood stories, and the waves breaking among the caves in the cliff had the solemn sound of sacred music.

When she got back, A-Mou would find her companions crouching in the darkness of the yard, singing while combing their hair. Some asked her hushed questions about what she had seen in the darkness. They talked of spirits. The blind women, their eyes open and unmoving in the shadows, seemed like visionaries of unknown and mysterious horizons.

A-Mou sat among them, stroking her guinea pig in her lap and listening, transfixed, to the tales of ghosts and witches that the old women, without hands, noses or ears, recited in solemn tones.

That was how she learnt that love was a dangerous thing. In the old women's stories, love, passion, betrothals, were always subject to adverse fortune, curses, tragic outcomes.

A-Mou had never loved, nor did she quite know what it was.

She had fallen ill as a young girl, and as a young girl she had ended up there, ignorant of life: and she was growing bored. But every evening, she was touched by emotion. As if she were to be told she was cured on the following day: a farewell party in the leper colony, with kisses and presents.

Yet, as she thought of the day of her resurrection, sitting there in the yard among her companions, she wondered what she would do afterwards. She had no family. Her grandmother, with whom she had fled from somewhere near Canton, had died soon after she had been interned there. She was a sad little old woman, with a greenish black velvet bonnet, who sat smoking opium for hours on end.

She remembered her grandmother's friends, who were also destitute: the elderly teacher, with his scrawny beard and learned words (she remembered poems he had taught her); the woman who sold snake oil by day, and at night spoke with the spirits of her ancestors.

Every morning, amid the clanging of saucepans in the kitchen, the sweetish smell of rice porridge in bowls in the refectory, dogs barking, A-Mou joyously greeted the sword of light that penetrated her alcove. In the mirror on her table, the blotches were still there on her cheekbones, sometimes pink, other times almost purple. But a new day beckoned. She had a lot to think about – plaiting her hair, seeing to her dress, waiting for the sun to go down.

Nor was she even aware of the arrival of the boy at the men's house, on the other side of the hill. The old women told how, one moonless night, he had crossed the river on a raft he had made himself. His condition wasn't serious. The doctor would put him right within a few months. He was a handsome boy.

A-Mou then began to imagine him as some sort of god, like the household deities at the entrance to the temple, brave, with birds on their shoulders, or like the evil spirit, who clutched a viper as if it were a sceptre – a god of terror as far as her grandmother was concerned, but whose beauty she, for her part, found seductive.

And so, without having tried to catch a glimpse of the new arrival, A-Mou found herself waiting for him all the time, and it was because of him that she took such care with her hair every day.

The boy, of course, would never come, for men were forbidden to invade the women's quarters, nor did she ever think of looking for him. But she thought of him in the morning, when she woke up, and during her evening walk, when she got dressed, and when she plaited her hair. She was convinced he had come especially to awaken her from the tedium of the passing hours.

Could it be that he knew of her existence? Surely, he must. Her grandmother used to say that threads of thought are stronger than those of a weaver. Thoughts could spin webs as long as imperial highways, capable of resisting typhoons, and crossing rivers and seas. She had thought so much about him that he knew all about her. And he had already committed himself to her.

Naturally, neither of them could expect anything lasting from each other. Once cured, if they happened to meet out there in the world of the healthy, they might pretend not to know one another. In the world of the healthy, nothing could be the same because they themselves would be different.

And she got to the point where she thought herself lucky for being ill, for their both being ill, for both rotting away there. What would become of him without her? What would become of her without him?

In the world of the healthy, they wouldn't need each other so much. Was that why God had sanctioned their illness… and their exile? In their misfortune, people became more important. Take her grandmother: at the end of her life, she never lacked the *white powder* for her pipe. And what a funeral the old teacher had had! The rich old woman of eighty who sat out in the main yard – surrounded by maids, and with no legs from the knees downwards – in health, she was just the mistress of her house; in sickness, she had the entire hospital at her beck and call.

Yes, indeed, misfortune had its compensations. In the world of the healthy, they would both lose their individuality. And she would never be as sure as she was now. The tales the old women told were of jealousy and betrayal. In their case, such things could never happen. Stories of folk who were free. Freedom had its price. Although she might not be able to count on his constancy later, A-Mou could count on him completely now.

And she thought about the boy with devotion, like someone whose thoughts dwelt on household gods, like someone recklessly worshipping the spirit of evil.

Time rushed by. Evenings merged into night. The women no longer included the matter of the new leper in their gossip. And A-Mou waited.

It was on one of her twilight walks that the dream became reality. Suddenly, when the sun had already set, she noticed a shape by her side, a shape that addressed her, told her his name, wanted to know hers. It could only be him. None of the patients, male or female, ever came there at that hour, and the healthy were filled with fear at the very sight of the lepers' hill. In the darkness, A-Mou could only see his eyes. The sea echoed among the hollows in the rocks. He plucked a sprig of lemon verbena from a nearby bush, crushed its leaves between his fingers, and the perfume spread and took hold of the night.

After that, it was more or less always the same. He would come after sunset. There was the scent of lemon and the sigh of the sea. On moonlit nights they managed to see each other perfectly. He complimented her on her plaited hair. She, in her heart, compared him to the young gods in the temple. The meetings repeated themselves, always the same, but always unexpected: the hours doubled their time; their silence expressed more than their words; their gesture was freely given; their soul was released.

But the months given by the doctor to cure the boy went by quickly. Could it be that he no longer had any blotches on his body? She was incapable of asking him, and without even wanting to know it, A-Mou saw hers grow, day by day, in the mirror.

As the women chatted in the evening, they now directed more questions at her.

And A-Mou had less and less to say.

When it came down to it, what was there to say? The purple

blotches on her face spoke for themselves, just as the legs she no longer had, spoke for the grand old lady who sat in the inner yard, and for others, hands, noses and ears. All faithfully resigned to their misfortune.

But how good it was that he had come to her on one, three, thirty nights. And how good it was that she, during all those nights, had believed in the apparition.

She still went for her evening walk to the top of the hill, but she no longer did so in order to contemplate the blaze of sunset, or to dream of a better tomorrow. Nor did she do so because of a man. She did it for herself alone. Because she had to live, in spite of being marked by death. Because the doctor had never again mentioned the possibility of a cure, and she needed to know about the joys of love in order to be able one day, crouching in the yard, to tell of them to some innocent young girl who might be sent to the leper colony.

THE PEDICAB DRIVER

The little boy child appeared one damp morning in March at the door of the convent. He was about six months old, light skinned, and with mixed Chinese and European features. A perfect child, wrapped in red flannel blankets and a charm made from bone on his wrist.

Naturally, the choir had to delay its prayers that morning. It was necessary to feed the child, who was crying loudly and sucking its thumb, and to change its cold damp clothes for warm dry ones. Bustle and enthusiasm among the younger nuns. Concern and pain on the solemn face of the mother superior.

It wasn't the first time abandoned children appeared at the doorway of the convent. But they were always newly born girls. Sometimes, the mothers went in person to offer them. Their parents didn't want them. They had to get rid of them in whatever way they could. The nuns tried to convince them otherwise, promising them food, clothing, but finally took the poor little creatures in, sending them to the crèche, from where, in due course, they would go on to the orphanage.

Some of these foundlings later converted and became nuns

themselves; others remained in the convent as servants, seamstresses. When they reached adulthood, they were given their lineage. They were called daughters of charity.

A boy, however, presented many more problems. Where would they put him after the crèche? For sure, the mother must be in a state of despair for having to abandon a boy child like that.

The maids would gossip among themselves: "What a travesty of a mother! A male child is the joy of any woman! She's a dancing woman for sure, a good time girl, no feelings in her soul, no honour."

The fat doorkeeper, the first one to see the boy, told them to hold their tongues. Who could tell why the mother had been led to reject her son? She had, indeed, taken care of him up until then… Who knew what lay behind the drama of such a separation? The only thing they could do was pray for her.

The mother superior, of course, never reported the matter to the authorities, nor did she try to find out the truth, for it would have been useless. It would be impossible to track down the family of the abandoned child in such a confused world, where most people had no identification papers. They were refugees from all corners of China, who arrived in large numbers day after day, and used false names. They knew nothing of each other, spoke different dialects, crowded together and hated one another, all living under the most tragic of possible fates: the lack of a piece of land.

Would the best solution then not be to adopt the foundling, baptize him, deliver him up to divine providence?

They gave him the name Francisco, in memory of the saint who had died over the water, on the adjacent island of Sanchuan, five hundred years before. His godmother was the oldest servant in the convent. His godfather was the saint.

But the day after the boy was found at the entrance to the convent, someone asked to see the mother superior in private. It was the pedicab driver, the man who shouted his fares across the square as the girls left college. He had come to ask for the boy to be given to him to care for, once the crèche could no longer keep him. He was old, poor, and alone in the world. But he yearned to look after someone. He had his sampan in the inner harbour, and there was room on it for the two of them. The fifty cents he got for every fare gave him enough at the end of the day for both of them.

The mother superior gladly accepted the proposal, on the condition that he attended the catholic church, catechism, and that the convent should look after his spiritual education.

The mother superior had prayed all night long to St Francis Xavier, asking for a home for the scorned child. The saint had promptly answered her prayers. A miracle. The old pedicab driver was a dependable Chinese, trusted by the convent. The little boy would be brought up among his own people. He would be baptized a Christian and educated in the Church. Who knows, he might become an example to many, and cause his own protector to seek conversion?

Francisco Cheong – the name was that of his adoptive parent – grew into a well-mannered choirboy, who helped at morning mass every day in the convent chapel, and at evening benediction, presented the priest with the censer.

Old Cheong would park his tricycle at the corner of the square, to go and watch the little boy in his acts of worship. Occasionally, a tear would come to his eye. The child looked more like an angel than a person. Silent steps to and fro in front of the altar, a bow followed by raised hands, the strange tongue he spoke, his red cassock getting in the way of his feet, the rustling of his lace ruff. How proud he was that fate had given him, a poor old man with no family, such a son, of mixed Chinese and European features, slim and fair skinned.

Then, he began to drop in at the temple to thank the gods for their gift of an adoptive son.

Francisco was intelligent. He did well in his studies. He wrote Chinese characters perfectly. He respected and loved the old man, whom he called father.

At the end of the afternoon, the pedicab driver stopped at the door of the boys' school. He didn't have to shout his fares there. He was coming to fetch Francisco who, books in hand, sat himself on the little seat after saying hello to his father. The man pedalled down the road, and both were happy as they made their way back to the boat on the muddy banks of the river.

In the morning, they made the journey up to the church, where the old man stood at the back of the nave, deeply touched by his son's bearing.

But the day came when a pious soul suggested to Francisco that he had a duty to bring his father into the bosom of Christ. There he was, a baptized Christian, a choirboy, a communicant, and his father frequented the temple, touching the floor with his forehead before Buddha, and consulting the fortune-teller. It wasn't right. How could he, a Catholic child grow up happily next to a father who worshipped idols?

Francisco had never been conscious of the problem before, and when it was put to him, it was somewhat reluctantly that he promised to approach his father concerning the matter. He found it difficult to bring up the subject, even disrespectful.

The old man took such pleasure in going to the temple on solemn feast days, in leaving offerings of food and burning incense at the altar of the gods! He had read in the old books that five hundred years before Christ, Goodness and Beauty were being preached in China. He could not distinguish greater virtues within himself as a Catholic than those of the old Buddhist.

It began on the journey back home, when darkness was falling. The boy watched his father's curved body pedalling away up front. He didn't know how to begin. The old man had never criticized his religion. On the contrary, he found it beautiful, and he felt pride when he saw him in the convent chapel helping the priest, lighting candles, and taking communion. Why should he now show scorn for his father's god, saying it was false, and that prayers and offerings to Buddha were worthless?

They arrived at home without exchanging a word.

Old Cheong wondered why the boy was so lost in thought that night.

There was an unusual silence over dinner. All that could be heard was the click of bamboo chopsticks against the side of the bowls. The old man offered him more rice. Francisco declined. Both of them sat in silence, gazing at the night and the dark waters. Then Francisco opened his mouth to recite a sentence from the Gospel. His father got up. The boat rocked. In the candlelight, the old man's shadow stretched like a bridge to the quay.

Finally, as they lay side by side on the rotting planks of the boat, the boy, taking courage from the darkness, broached the subject of religion.

The old man listened attentively. He liked to hear his son talk. How knowledgeable the lad was! Of course he didn't understand all he was saying. But God seemed an excellent topic of conversation.

Francisco told him about the mysteries of his faith, and referred to the Bible, and the stages in the life of Jesus.

Sleepiness weighed heavily on the pedicab driver's tired eyelids: a good tiredness, lulled by his son's words, words full of sweetness, pardon, and love.

It was growing late, and the moon was rising. A full, milky moon that the boy contemplated as he went on talking, and which brought to his mind the memory of some deity – Our Lady? A saint? The Spirit of Night? –"… Peace on Earth and good will to all men," he murmured.

And he compared divine peace to the fullness of the moon. He felt such peace as he had never felt before. And he didn't say any more.

Next to him, bathed in moonlight, his eyes closed, silent, it was as if his father were dead. So pure and good! He wanted to caress his hands gently. His soul must surely look like the face of the moon. Religion, God, prayer, were they not enshrined in the old man with the pure soul, just like the moon and its serenity, which radiated from both?

Yet no one had taught him such a doctrine. He hadn't learned it in catechism or at school. Maybe the teachers and priests had never noticed the moon or the pedicab driver. But he now knew how it really was. That night had been a revelation to him. Neither Christians, nor Buddhists, nor Taoists, nor Confucionists… there was only one God. A god of all people.

The old man opened his eyes again with difficulty, overcoming sleep. His son was silent, contemplative; no doubt he had finished his beautiful story. And Cheong stuttered:

"So young and knowing things an old man scarcely understands! That's why I go to the temple after leaving you in the nuns' chapel. I must thank the gods for such a son!"

RACIAL HATRED

Although he was getting on in years, the rich man kept up his habit of taking a new wife every new moon. Tai-Ku – his eldest daughter – thought he was ill. How innocent she was!

One by one, her sisters had left, dressed in red and gold, and wearing their nuptial headdress, for their husbands' homes. Tai-Ku had remained. She had remained in order to warm the great man's bath every morning, to pour his tea, to forgive him his lasciviousness.

Tai-Ku was in effect a Buddhist holy woman. If she had not shaved her head, nor changed her silk dress for one of coarse wool, it was because her father would not agree to it. She lived for prayers, fasting, and leaving her offerings at the altar.

Tai-Ku ignored every woman who crossed the courtyards of the house. Every one of them was a virgin. He insisted on their being untouched. Then they became his protégées, and he would shower them with gifts, indulge them.

Tai-Ku thought it was because he was ill. Never once did her lips open to censure him, nor did she ever concern herself with family, neighbours or friends; it did not matter to her whether the rich man had five hundred or eight hundred women.

Every morning, Tai-Ku would impassively go and feel the temperature of her father's bath water. Her duties had caused her hair to grow white. She trod noiselessly over the mosaic of the courtyards, in her slippers made from rice straw. As first daughter, she carried out her filial duties, without seeking to know who the new wife was, without wishing her ill, or showing any interest in making her acquaintance.

Of the world in which her father and the other people lived, she only had one recollection – and that was a terrible one. Crestfallen, she had chosen exile within herself.

Once, the Japanese had been there. They had passed through and stayed. She was only a young girl then. Her mother was dying in childbirth, and she was buried without flowers, without priests to commend her soul to Buddha. Weeds were growing in the streets. The Japanese installed themselves in the house, taking over its rooms and women servants. Her father ceded part of his fleet of ships to them to avoid it being destroyed completely, and surrendered his jewels in order not to have to surrender his daughters.

Tai-Ku hated those Japanese. She had witnessed their insolence right there in her own home. She had watched them mistreat the people, scorn the Law, desecrate the temple. She detested those Japanese more than all the satanic spells put together. From that time, she had never stopped beseeching the Heavens to inflict all manner of punishment on them.

Tai-Ku, the innocent. That's what the servants called her, but it was her father who had given her the title.

When he received a new wife every new moon, the rich man would make offerings of perfume and gold to his eldest daughter's God. He held her in greater love than he did himself. He had great respect for his daughter's wisdom, her purity. He believed she was a saint.

However, no one was aware of the hatred that had infiltrated Tai-Ku's soul during the Japanese occupation. She had kept it hidden, and her heart nurtured it in solitary silence, just as the desert soil incubates the eggs of a viper. It was the dark fruit of her colourless days, and Tai-Ku felt it ripen in every prayer she said, every fast, every sacrifice made to the Eternal one. Sometimes, it seemed to her as if it was all she had left. It took over her whole life. It gnawed away at her insides, consuming her.

One winter's day, Wa-Lai, her maid, hinted that there was a new concubine.

Tai-Ku was lighting candles on the altar to her ancestors, indifferent to the old woman's gossip. However, the grating of a certain word alarmed her. The servant was talking about a Japanese woman.

Japanese?

For several nights after that, she was unable to sleep. Her past kept returning: her mother dying a lonely death (from fright?), the cries of the servants, the soldiers marching across the courtyards. They belonged to yesterday, today, tomorrow, they were of all time. She had only lived that instant, but it had become eternal. Nothing had ever happened before or since. Ever. And for the first time, she rebelled. She had found God, it was true, but she had never found herself. Was she so enmeshed in her bitterness? Her soul was divided, like that of someone who served both Good and Evil.

At night, she lay awake. By day, she ran a fever, and laughed.

In her father's quarters, there was music and singing. She had even listened, hidden by the branches of the jackfruit tree in the main courtyard.

Wa-Lai had said that the Japanese girl had a slim face, as transparent as the flesh of a lemon, and that her voice recalled the song of a bird and a flower. His lordship would love her more than any other. Japanese women, with their slanting eyes, were queens of love. This one sang and played.

Tai-Ku knew for sure that her father hated the Japanese, like any Chinese worth his salt. But a woman had no nationality, as far as he was concerned. The great man needed a new young girl each new moon, and money allowed him to choose as the mood took him: adolescents with fresh young bodies and chaste eyes, defenceless against lasciviousness, or fully grown women, pulsating with eagerness and desire. Women of all types and every nationality. But a Japanese... No. She, Tai-Ku, the eldest daughter couldn't put up with so much.

That evening, Tai-Ku carried out her usual tasks distractedly: she checked the money spent that day, gave orders for the following day, cut out rice paper flowers for the festivities in the temple, and prayed. However, she paid no attention to what she was doing, focusing obsessively on a matter closer to hand. And a plan began to develop in her mind, gradually, as if inevitable. A Japanese indeed!

Of all the hundreds of women her father had had, she had never wanted to even know their names. But when this one arrived, she was the target for preconceived ideas.

With her nimble hands, Tai-Ku made snow white crowns out

of the petals of the jasmine flower, to which were fixed shoots of orange blossom and pressed lotus leaves… And the Japanese woman was right there. The Japanese woman was taking over her heart and mind, even stealing the place reserved for God!

The flowers fell from her lap, fluttering to the mosaic floor like paper, where they spread out as if on a grave. Tai-Ku shivered.

Her religion taught her not to kill. But did it not also tell her to expunge evil? And didn't the Japanese woman incarnate the worst of all evils – violence, war… and the inferno inside her heart?

She spent seven sleepless nights, and then decided. She pondered on how to do it. She wouldn't know how to handle a weapon.

Was it a sin to destroy her enemy? Surely it was a sin for the invader's daughter to be living in the house her forefathers had violated, to be occupying the bed where the legitimate wife had died in terror, with no flowers on her grave, or priests to direct her soul towards Buddha. It was a sin for the Japanese woman to be living there, right next to her hatred.

The moon was rising, round and yellow like an orange, and Tai-Ku was awake. She had grown thin. She was livid. Oh! If only she could kill her with the poison from her heart! Then an idea inflamed her mind, penetrating every twist and turn, every crevice of her being. The cavern of her mind was now clear and light. Her fears were swept aside. Tai-Ku could now see all that she had to do, as clearly as she could see the branches of the jackfruit tree, like human arms, hugging the moonlit night.

Chinese New Year was approaching. The sprigs of peach blossom, the pale chrysanthemums, the dwarf tangerine trees in terracotta pots, all the symbols of happiness which Tai-Ku used to give her father on those days, no longer interested her. Tai-Ku was thinking about the snake. She had zealously ordered it for the new year dinner. Snake was always suitable for a supper in winter, along with swallows' nests, and Peking-style duck. She would prepare everything herself. She would extract their livers for balm against fever. She would have wine made from the bile.

That day, she had a wry smile on her face. The servants were puzzled. Tai-Ku was normally such a serious girl. The gold-capped teeth, which usually glinted in brief polite smiles, now surprised them, permanently gleaming in the slender mouth of their master's eldest daughter.

The snake. She would be able to sleep at long last. She could calm down. Her mother was avenged. And the echoes through the great house. And *her*. Her pulse raced as if she were in love. Within her, all was celebration. Celebration and terror.

The snake. The tiny pouch full of poison slid into her shiny leather bag. No one had noticed. Her father would congratulate her for the snake soup with its chrysanthemum petals, with its lemon leaves. He would enjoy the wine. Of course, the concubines would not be dining with the family. Tai-Ku would make sure some of the festive drink was sent to the Japanese woman. Tai-Ku would see to everything.

Firecrackers were going off in the streets. Perhaps after all this, she really would go mad. She felt as if the inside of her head were about to explode. She was in a fluster. Her soul was screaming and she could feel the force of her screams against her temples. Life was giddily taking possession of her entire being, while at the same time suffocating her. Maybe in the end, she would find peace.

But then, suddenly, the old master was anxiously calling out for her. Tai-Ku was taken unawares. Her father. Would her father suffer greatly as a result of her vengeance? Could it be that he really loved the Japanese woman? One of the main precepts of the Buddhist doctrine concerned filial piety. Her father! And she rushed to find him.

Something terrible had happened. The Japanese woman had died suddenly, she had been found dead in her bed on New Year's morning, purple, her eye sockets bloodied. (Her father spoke, slowly, with difficulty.) The geisha who took such exquisite care in bathing his feet, who entertained him by singing in the gentlest voice in the world, had suddenly ceased to live, struck down by some mysterious illness.

With downcast eyes, Tai-Ku listened to the news. Then, she sat with her father at dinner. It was Sunday. There were stewed chicken giblets. The old man's hands trembled like bamboo in the wind, as he held his ivory chopsticks, and his seventy odd years weighed upon him. Tai-Ku pitied him. From one moment to the next, he had become decrepit: his eyes were sunken, his skin dull, his shoulders hunched.

He asked her to help him get ready for bed. And he remained in bed for three days. In fact, he never got up again.

At the dying man's bedside, Tai-Ku was like a statue. Her father asked her to sit at the foot of the bed so that he could look at her. He didn't want anyone else in the room, except for her, right to the end. His eldest daughter. His daughter, who had never stood in the way of his habits, never criticized his excesses. Tai-Ku, the innocent one.

A great peace emanated from Tai-Ku's pale face. Her father contemplated her. Never before had he found her so beautiful. Why had Tai-Ku never married? The best, most gifted of his daughters. Had her dedication, her devotion to the Divine one, been any compensation? In truth, who but a god would have deserved her? And the veneration he had always felt for her now grew into limitless love that filled his heart to overflowing, and stifled him. And this love redeemed him from all the base passions of his life.

With her eyes half closed, Tai-Ku tried to pray. But she couldn't even order her thoughts. Her spirit was now so free, that it was as if it no longer existed, or existed far far away, outside her being, as if it were crossing the darkened paths of absence, in order to become re-united with her father in the great Unknown.

THE CHILD OF THE SUN

The cold always arrived suddenly, straight after Christmas night. One would go to Midnight Mass still wearing silk. In the college one was offered hot tea and sesame buns after the three masses – in the main hall, presents lying at the feet of the Baby Jesus on the stage, which had been turned into a stable. The only people who remained were the girls from poor families, those who had no family to go to over the holidays, the odd solitary teacher.

The director, an American nun, distorted her name as she called her. She smiled and went over. It was a little parcel wrapped in bright red paper and tied with a gold ribbon. Later she remembered brushing her lips against a cold surface. Could it have been a kiss of peace and goodwill deposited on the bony face of the elderly director? Or was it Baby Jesus' ivory feet?

She got a bead necklace that made her think of a rattle. She blushed as she realized the implications of her thought.

"Why is it that everyone's staring at me? The girls… as if they'd never seen me before… I'm feeling dizzy. And what if I faint?"

In the exposed emptiness of the hall, lit by the candles from the Nativity Scene, the tiny group of teachers and pupils, part inhibited and part hostile, mingled with difficulty.

Father Matthew, the Franciscan from Scotland, made a vain attempt to practise his Cantonese with the girls.

Sister Chen-Mou emerged from inside, her moonlike face glowing, with some ginger sweets on a china dish. The girls pressed round her. They showed her their presents and asked her the time.

Then, everything returned to normal. In the dull flickering of the candles, people's faces seemed strangely elongated.

On the mosaic floor, the design of the cross stood out clearly, while the ceiling, the walls, the doors were swallowed up by the darkness of night.

What a fright he had given her at that hour as he emerged from the shadow of the birch trees along the side of the road! She had quickened her pace ever since leaving the square. Her heart was throbbing. She had almost fainted right there at his feet.

The man smelt vaguely of sandalwood. He apologized politely for frightening her. In fact he was going the same way as she was. At the institute there had been a Christmas party because the rector was a converted Christian. Six pupils had been baptized. Both Christian and Buddhist teachers had been present. They had drunk rice wine and burnt incense sticks.

The road was steep and he offered her his arm, but she rejected it. Dogs barked. He said he was sorry he didn't have a car to give her a lift home. He talked about Chinese New Year, which would be at the next full moon. They could go and buy a sprig of peach blossom together. He smiled. She wasn't listening to him, absorbed as she was in one thought alone: the child of his she was carrying.

"How many moons ago? Sometimes it seems as if so much time has passed... as if it was in another life".

In another life... The two of them alone and fearful of being so. Alone with Nature: clear skies, leafy trees, bodies, light, long, smooth. And a joy that was pure, like childhood.

They were passing the cemetery. The owl hooted. She instinctively moved closer to him. She felt like crying, crying long and loud.

Her homeland was on the other side of the world. There was snow. Her family must be giving her a special thought on that night. And maybe they were writing to her, sending her presents. The food they would be eating there, the clinking of glasses, the uninhibited banter, laughter, exclamations. The family! She would never be able to see them again. In her belly she bore the blood of a different race, the child of someone she had never known or loved (someone born thousands of years before), the false, hybrid fruit of her own shamelessness.

She suddenly felt hugely sorry for the man. He was so intelligent! And tall and distinguished. A northern Chinese? A nobleman among the coarse little Cantonese. She felt sorry too for his complete ignorance of what she alone knew and hid from him: yet it was a mystery that was impossible without him. She felt sorry for her treachery, for her vengeance.

"And what if it was good for him tonight?"

The Moon had risen. Thinner than ever, the cypresses in the cemetery cast their shadow diagonally over the side of the road. His shadow was just like that of the cypresses. That plant-like aroma... She began to listen to him. He was speaking Mandarin. He spoke in verses. Exotic and musical, like the wind blowing through a thicket of bamboos. His hand open like a palm leaf.

No. One couldn't love a gesture, a sound, a myth. And he was only a gesture, sound, myth. No matter how much she tried, she couldn't remember anything real, physical. It all blended into the aridity of spirit, languidly vague and melancholic – a landscape of sand...

Once, in a bar, they were drinking cocktails. There was a Chinese clock between drapes of glass beads. But time didn't exist. With him, it was always outside time. His narrow eyes spoke of painful, distant corners of eternity. Those lips moistening her, the puff of his breath against her skin. Cold lips, like the ivory feet of the Baby Jesus in the Nativity scene.

On another occasion, she had wanted to caress him. It was a hot August afternoon. On the horizon, boats with the black half-moon shapes of their sails. He smiled, a distant smile like those in portraits. She was left with the sensation of having caressed the face of the wind.

Then there was the lesson in the main hall on graduation day. There he was dressed formally in purple and black, in the old imperial style. The foreign language gushing from his dry lips, perfectly, eloquently. The paleness of his face. He was a prince, a wise man. She was drawn to the abyss by his intellectual power. Her senses were confused. She felt the sensual pleasure of that which cannot be explained.

She couldn't have that child. She hadn't felt it taking shape from her flesh. She was absent from its gestation. She had conceived it unnaturally out of his spirit, just as the first woman in the world, according to Confucius, had conceived from her own shadow.

She knew morning had already long broken because she heard the cry of the tricycle drivers on the road in the distance. She knew it was Christmas because she could see the little parcel in its scarlet paper on the table.

She wrapped her padded silk jacket around her chest. The cold had arrived, religiously punctual on Christ's birthday.

In the centre of the city, there were stalls selling trinkets and junk – the usual buzz of the crowd, accentuated by the Christian festival. On the food stalls, pork crackled in boiling oil, lotus seeds, bean shoots and bamboo shoots, watermelon seeds, fried rice, fried noodles. On the street corners, the blind read fortunes with trembling fingers. The old organ grinder and seller of remedies uttered her incomprehensible ditty. The pedicab drivers shouted their way through the crowds.

Almost unconsciously, she went into the temple. As always, there were devotees burning paper offerings among the smoking ashes. Some were touching the ground with their forehead before the Buddha and others respectfully rang the bell to bring their sufferings to the attention of the placid divinity.

The Chinese shuffled the fortune sticks around in the bamboo cup, and told her to choose one. He took a dusty roll of parchment down from the wall and began to read.

She listened attentively.

The air was pungent, thick with smoke.

The priest said that she had been born under a moon swept by the east winds, which promised both good fortune and risks, but that the Goddess of Anxiety was watching over her fate, because no god knew her horoscope. He added that she confused heavenly values with those of the earth, and that was the root of her perdition, that she possessed nothing because she had wanted everything, that hers was a truly unusual destiny.

The Chinese looked like the Buddha on the altar: his shaven head gleamed, and his smile was enigmatic, serene, other worldly.

She slowly climbed the steps of the college. The director received visitors in the locutory. Chinese couples, solemn and ceremonious, came and went with their children in tow. Prelates. Superiors from other schools. On a little camphor table, bowls of tea and soya flour cakes coloured with vermilion.

She had come to say goodbye.

The director's eyes glazed with astonishment.

She presented her apologies, deep down proud of the lies she was telling with such conviction, while she assessed the surprise in the director's eyes, imagining how glassy they would become if she were to confess the only thing worth confessing: the truth in which she herself didn't believe.

"How many moons ago was it? It was autumn. Autumn here is reminiscent of spring: warm, clear, scented. And how happy we were! Naturally, and for no special reason. Just happy. Happy like the earth when the sun covers it. Why don't I shout it out? Happy and beautiful!"

The director sat fidgeting in her large armchair. She summoned the deputy director.

Muffled steps crossed the paved courtyard. The deputy director wore dark glasses.

She was asked to start all over again. But she felt terribly tired. She felt like telling it from the end to the beginning, like keeping quiet, like asking them to do the talking.

The director talked about the Child in the stable, about his beauty.

But what did her child have to do with that?

In the public garden the shadows of the trees began to extend along the paths. The bell of the nuns' chapel rang – The Birth of Christ. The temple – the priest's words. Her God. His God. She had resorted to both and she had to reach her decision alone. Hers inspired such a deep fatigue that it was as if she were already dead.

In the inner harbour, the shifting city of junks and sampans – muddy hulks, bare masts like fingers against the sky – contained all the ancientness of the world.

She stood watching the paper kites fluttering merrily in the deep red of the sunset. The kites tied to the piles of the quay. She became entangled in their nylon threads. The threads of pain that tied her to life.

"It was in the autumn and it seemed like spring. I don't think I loved him but I was happy. We were both happy. What did it matter that it was only for an instant? He deserved to be loved…"

Night descended. All was darkness.

Oh! If only someone could stay and tell of such joy! If only there were someone who could say that she had been there and was carrying in her belly a child of the sun!

FERNANDA DIAS

She was born in the southern Alentejo, Portugal, and has lived in Macau since 1986. A printer, engraver and graphic artist, whose work has been exhibited in Macau, she is the author of two collections of poems, *Horas de Papel* (1992) and *Rio de Ehru* (1999), and a collection of short stories, *Dias da Prosperidade* (1998). She has more poetry and stories at press, including renderings in Portuguese of Chinese poems. She teaches at the Portuguese School in Macau.

THE WATERMELON

It is raining. A never-ending, warm drizzle. The hotel is full of tourists, actors in a film with no plot. Girls dressed in red and pink nylon lacework, adorned with bows, strings of plastic pearls, tiny hats squeezing their plaits, crowd into the elevators. Their tiny, restless feet reveal rough socks with stiff tassels and patent leather shoes, buckled on the side.

Our room is on the east wing, eighteenth floor. I go over to the window. In the distance, the fresh green of the rice paddies is like a watercolour with its delicately changing tones, behind the glass of the window. The hotel is isolated in its excessive height. The city is huge and spread out.

China, China, I murmur to myself, my face leaning against the coolness of the windowpane. A-Fai examines the brash *fin-de-siècle* décor of the room. He gets undressed, and settles down to watch television. Out there, the large but small city stretches away below me like a huge tapestry embroidered with bamboo hats, and innumerable bicycle wheels, spinning dizzily along.

This is the China whose ground I tread, smell, kiss, observe with eyes brimming with an inexplicable sadness, and breathe in great gulps of air, this is China, with its wet rice stalks, ginger flower, blue window frames, crude umbrellas, priestly buffaloes, warm mud, flaming banana trees, straw huts, and its multitude of eyes that stare at me, like black stars on the dull surface of their faces.

In the afternoon we go for a walk through the town, totally alien in its almost rural bustle. Everything buzzes, whistles, tinkles, snorts: motor vehicles, bicycles, tricycles, long poles carried over shoulders, laden with firewood, bamboo, fruit, poultry in cages, baskets, tools.

Faint wisps of smoke swathe the windows, with their whimsical ironwork no doubt salvaged from some nearby foundry, in a type of resinous mystery.

I glance discreetly into the kitchens at street level. Apprehensively, I take in the harmony of the place, where every object, polished by daily use, has its own particular beauty. The diligent, swift, silent hands, of women, children, old people, have touched those pans, those benches, those stoking irons. All those materials that time has ennobled, clay, bamboo, wood, iron, have clattered and rung with the same familiar voices through countless similar days, and have become imbued with the sound of names, which are the stamp and hallmark of every family.

By the doorways, old men sit meditatively on their granite seat, with their hookah between their legs.

A-Fai walks beside me, his forgotten camera slung over his shoulder, brushing against his denim jacket.

> "I used to sit and play on a bench like that when I was a child, in the yard of my grandmother's house. These places take me back to the past. You just can't imagine what a

beautiful town Macau was. It was so quiet..."

Some sort of grey, dank sadness emanates from the clean, flower-lined narrow street. We reach a muddy river. Dark boats glide along, loaded with mud coloured bundles. An old woman, leaning on a balcony overlooking the river, spits into the waters. Everything has the colour, the warm, fluid placidity of a dream. I answer:

"When I was a child, I imagined China to be covered in gardens full of bamboo and peonies, lakes with herons, pagodas, girls with painted silk sunshades and bound feet, frowning warriors clad in bronze and jade armour."

A-Fai laughs, puts his arm round my shoulder, and says to me as he leads me on:

"Come and see China..."

We pass through a maze of narrow lanes, clean, damp, deserted, hieroglyphic black bicycles leaning against high garden walls. I think of the China Pessanha spoke of, the China *of garishly dressed mandarins, excessive in their pomp and vanity, of interminable formalities and courtesies in their daily intercourse, tedious in its cringing servility, and consisting of feigned solicitude and hyperbolic adulation... of ruinous luxury, in the service of ostentatious prodigality, in funeral ceremonies, weddings, banquets...* of brutal pirates, squalid beggars, corrupt magistrates, sadistic executioners, sinister eunuchs, beautiful ladies with mutilated feet and cruel souls weaving intrigues in the harems. I am forbidden to speak of this China, under risk of putting my finger on an ancient and painful sore.

We pause in a quiet square. There is a long wall with high windows, and an open gate. A deserted courtyard. The silence is vibrant and crystalline, as if inhabited by the echoes of recent voices. On the walls, there are large posters in bright colours, smiling children, surrounded by artless flowers and patriotic exhortations. A-Fai's strong arms lift me up so that I can see through the barred window. I see a huge, brick-floored room, with rows of tiny wooden benches, darkened with age. From the ceiling hang paper decorations.

There is a strange, pervasive beauty about the place. Delicate as a bud and fragile as a wisp of incense smoke, the smell of chalk comes back to me, vivid and disturbing, of blackboards and old books, of sweaty pinafores. The smell of time gone by. Very slowly, A-Fai deposits me on the worn brickwork of the huge yard. I find myself saying:

"It's not only your childhood in there, it's also mine…"

We have dinner in a floating restaurant on the river, known for its fried quail. It's already late and the dining room is almost empty. Girls in red gowns work hard to serve us the best dishes. I take some photos, knowing full well that with the passing of time they will turn into the hard, gleaming stiletto we call pain and memory.

On our way back to the hotel we pass through a smoke filled evening market. Refreshment stalls display just about anything one could imagine eating and drinking, along with appropriate drinks, beer, soya milk, *pou-lei* tea, cane syrup, chrysanthemum tea. As we pass the fruit stalls, A-Fai says:

"Why don't we buy a watermelon to take back to the hotel? We can eat it later tonight, while we watch television."

"Good idea", I reply. I choose one, heavy, with a split down the side, scented like a night in an orchard. Through the crack, I glimpse cool, juicy flesh, pure carmine in a jade cup. The fruit seller puts it in a yellow plastic bag and passes it to me. A-Fai has finished paying, gets his change, while I wait for him to put his wallet away and hold the bag out to him, with the melon inside.

"You carry it," he says, as he starts walking again.

"No you take it, it's heavy."

He walks on without looking back. It's obvious he doesn't want to carry the watermelon. I just need to know why. I follow him, still holding the bag out with both hands.

"And why should I carry it? Can you tell me?" To which he replies:

"You carry it, and that's that."

"I don't want to carry it. It's heavy and it's hurting my hand."

I follow him, thinking that perhaps I should sulk and drop the bag on the ground. But if I do that, he will be so angry that I'll never be able to ask him why he doesn't want to carry the watermelon. And I'll have to give up trying to understand.

I drag my feet, like a pregnant woman. I hug the watermelon with both arms, the yellow bag next to my stomach. Questions come to my mind like pieces in an unfamiliar puzzle.

What secret taboo inhibits him from walking though the market with a watermelon?

Or rather, what sort of prejudiced pride is it that stops him walking beside a western woman, and carrying fruit in a plastic bag?

Or again, what lesson does he want to teach me, obliging me to follow him, heavily loaded, when he, who is walking ahead with such a sure step, his hands free, could lift the bag with his little finger?

And what strange shame is it that makes me refrain from pressing home my question? What ancestral instinct is it that compels me to abandon my impulse to leave the bag by the wayside?

Night is falling, and now that everybody has left work, the number of passers-by increases. They look at us and smile at me. I don't know why but I seem to detect in their eyes a spark of sympathy, but which is not devoid of mischief. I return their smile, as if to say: "I don't really mind carrying this bloody watermelon."

I raise the yellow bag up to my breasts. Darkness now falls, vanquishing any resistance. I enter the hotel proudly hoisting my watermelon aloft, as if it were a flag of surrender.

THE ROOM

I remember that as I passed by the huge dustbins I saw two swift, fat, sleek rats. The strange tense movement that precedes the sudden rush with which rats scuttle along had always attracted my attention. But A-Fai doesn't understand my curiosity for such sordid reality.

Entering a narrow alleyway, we would turn left, and I would walk along as if in a dream over rotten wooden planks, which crossed in unchanging pattern the puddle of dirty water coming from the rear of an eating establishment. I never discovered the corresponding front entrance, lost among the endless labyrinth of little factories and businesses behind the harbour. Workshops, with wide doorways under arcades, made cables, oars, rope, boxes, tubs, mended machines, cars, bicycles, sold in small quantity or in bulk incense sticks, firecrackers, tobacco, Chinese medicines, tea, tools, drinks, cassette recordings of Peking opera and Hong Kong crooners. And at any hour, food was made and served in quite astounding quantities.

For this reason, the bustle in the little inner courtyard never really died down: women and men crouched over large tubs to wash the blue and white crockery used everyday, huge cooking pots, yellow clay dishes, blackened and shiny inside, wire colanders, iron woks and plastic chopsticks. And depending on the time and the season, prepared different types of food: seaweed, prawns, sharks' fins, crabs trussed up with reeds, dried or live fish, fresh or pickled vegetables, freshly killed or lacquered poultry, and a thousand and one other things unknown to me, but whose shape, texture, viscosity and smell caused me to stop in my tracks and increase my intake of breath. But A-Fai, keeping his beautiful hand, the colour of raw silk, on my shoulder, propelled me gently forward, in what was nothing less than the outward demonstration of an irresistible force.

We climbed some dirty wooden stairs and, on the landing cluttered with bits of disused furniture, with speed and precision he would open a door made of iron bars and garlanded with bits of old cloth, then another wooden one, which was bolted and chained, and we would enter a tiny, rectangular room, with two narrow, barred windows in the wall opposite the door. I imagine these looked out over rooftops onto the Rua Almirante Sérgio, but I was never able to verify this. Under one of them, there was a desk covered with papers and any number of objects, all coated in a layer of dust, whose varying degree of thickness indicated the length of time they had been there: a key ring from Rome, pens of every description, a cigarette lighter from the "Nam Kuong", a fake gold elephant from Thailand. Coins from China and Canada, newspaper cuttings, spare parts from Japanese electrical goods, invitations to exhibitions at the City Council, receipts from the "Royal Gymnasium". I looked at all this, perplexed, for I knew, I sensed that they were the icons of some unknown religion. Later, I would have occasion to analyze the meaning of each one, for they all formed part of some strange, barbaric myth, and it is all I have left now. Today, I have all these objects at home, clean, tidied away, as if they were the possessions of some forgotten god in a museum.

To the left of the door, over a plastic settee, there was a huge framed poster of James Dean in black and white, with his famous Egyptian amulet round his neck. To the right of the door, in a little glass fronted cupboard, one could see beautiful little models of Napoleonic soldiers lined up, on foot and on horseback, startlingly realistic models of Second World War tanks, and fearful in their dynamic ranks, an impressive crowd of heroes and robots from Japanese comics. Everything tiny and flimsy, everything assembled and coloured in with precision and dedication, a testament to an ardent but solitary adolescence.

With an enthusiastic glint in his eyes, he showed me his fragile treasure, he rolled the rarer pieces in the palm of his hand, showing me the painstaking techniques employed to assemble them, the secret use of the enamel paints, while listing the prizes awarded by the City Council in school competitions.

There was also a plastic wardrobe, where he carefully kept his jeans, his immaculate white tee-shirts, and his American cadet style jackets. Then there were two narrow iron bedsteads, separated at their head by a bookcase, bulging with magazines such as *Man Club*, *Esquire*, along with Japanese and Hong Kong comics, all carefully arranged and protected with plastic covers, on which there was not even a speck of dust. The beds were also clean, with their straw mats the colour of old gold, and their padded cotton blankets, neatly folded next to the wall, which at this point was covered in a plastic sheet of imitation tiles.

Objects often suffer a strange exile: over A-Fai's bed, opposite the second window, there was an American flag, given him by a passing sailor friend, its stars glittering.

Although I had often stayed there until late at night, seated on the bed with A-Fai, looking at comics, or swapping untranslatable snippets of memory with him, I never met the friend who slept in the other bed.

One summer night, we locked the door and lay naked, our bodies entwined under the weak current of cool air produced by the fan. Of an indefinite colour, perched on top of a stool between the two beds, the fan whirred, shrouded in a fluttering cloud of grime, which gave it the air of some creature from another world. There was a knock on the door, but A-Fai, placing his hand gently over my lips, told me to remain quiet and didn't answer it. We heard a second brushing of fingers against the wood, and nothing else. No one called, there was no clearing of a throat, nor did I hear steps on the creaking planks of the old staircase. Even now, I don't know whether it was a man or a woman, a visitor or someone who had come to stay. Maybe it was a common occurrence – his friend came and, finding the door locked, withdrew discreetly. Or it was some mysterious lover, who went away with an anxious heart.

I never asked him about it. Apart from this, he told me so many things spontaneously, opened up his memory to me with such passion, that I could only listen to him religiously! In return, I allowed to slip from myself an ancient torrent of words and tales, of Gilgamesh and Enkidu, Baketamon and the captain of the guard at Amenhotep, Morgana the fairy and the Hoofed Lady, Prince Pedro and Inês, the Licorn Lady and the Long Awaited King. Using words from three languages, mine, his and a rudimentary English, we invented a language of our own, as effective as a trap, and we became ever more ensnared by it.

Occasionally, I began to imagine myself tipping all his junk onto the landing, and scrubbing down his room with plenty of soap and water, along with all it contained, after which I would put everything back in its place, minus its dark film of dust and grime. A-Fai would brood when I tried to put this plan into action, and one Sunday in May, he bluntly made me promise not to mention cleaning that hateful place ever again.

There was a wooden shelf over the beds where he kept his boxes of models, many of them still unassembled. This space, which lessened the height of an already low room, obliged him to bend his head and shoulders, and he looked like Atlas, weighed down by the burden of an invisible world. He spoke of the room as a place of temporary condemnation. He would take off his clothes, fold them carefully, and fill that limited space with the living splendour of his statuesque body. He looked after his muscles like someone carrying out a ritual, but he didn't believe in the beauty of his face. The American cinema stereotype mocked the sleeping Narcissus within him. But there was I, all eyes, to witness the mystery of such harmony, to suffer the anguish of the solitary contemplation of beauty. Those who felt the same unremitting pain included Jean Genet, the martyr, Yukio Mishima, the aesthete, and Boris Vian, my hero.

A-Fai looked at himself in the mirror through its archipelago of smudges, and talked to himself. His pure, young body seemed incorruptible. It was for that reason, that purpose, that I was there. To make of him the focal point of a dream. In front of the mirror, the subtle tone of his voice gave expression to the ancient, inflected, antediluvian mother of all languages.

His face, which I didn't dare to look at for any length of time except in rash moments or when he was asleep, revealed to me the mystery of those ancient Buddhas whose body has the vegetable qualities of the lotus plant, and whose smile is the last crimson ray of the Sun as it sinks into the Sea.

TENANTS

It takes five or twenty minutes to get from S. Lázaro to Mitra by way of the footbridge over the Rua do Campo, depending on how fast you walk, and the length of your step. Normally I walk quickly and don't get tired, but I've done that journey so often, carrying granny Sok-I's bamboo case bursting with books, clothes and the innumerable things one takes when moving house, that it has become a sort of *via sacra*, with certain obligatory stops, the first on the corner by the old library, the second at the beginning of the Rua do Pato, at the point where a paving stone serves as a bench outside a tiny house, its grey brickwork still visible under years of paint, and garlanded with clothes drying on a bamboo pole. Once I have passed the "Vencedora" eating house, I pause in the little temple to To-Tei, the old guide to the gods who lose their way while travelling earthly roads. In the quiet interior, softened by the smoke from incense sticks and the fine veil of ash from burnt votive slips, I ask the bearded Old Man, smiling between Wife and Concubine: will I be able to live on the threshold of the unknown? Will I be able to accept what I can't understand? Will I learn how to cook rice? For I'm a stranger admitted into the most intimate recess of urban life. As if love were nothing more than a conventional pretext to enter a labyrinth to which each one of us is the door.

I hadn't liked the apartment. One entered the building through a narrow doorway, which would no longer be noticeable once the construction company's painted board, perched on a bamboo structure, had been taken away. We went there for the first time one winter afternoon. It smelt of fresh concrete and paint, a smell I would forever associate with my passion and joy at having discovered intimacy with the other. Looking upwards all around us, we saw the small square of windows, some already with grilles added, and far away, as if at the end of an inverted well, the white sky. Down below, on the concrete floor of the courtyard, some recently planted dwarf palm trees began their exile arranged in a square formation of pots.

The elevator, with its stencilled design in sky-blue, had a strident bell that announced each floor. At night, its sinister echo will reverberate down empty corridors, I thought to myself for no particular reason. And I said:

> "The two bedroom windows look onto a gloomy yard; from that tiny balcony in the living room, you can see into the neighbours'."

But he sat down on the cheap sofa, passed his hand over its pink and grey check pattern, stroking this domestic object as if it were alive. He considered it a minor inconvenience to have one's space cluttered by furniture, with its false Italian design in white lacquer, and he let out a deep sigh, or rather a brief, muffled grunt, like an animal settling down in his warm lair after a troubled, errant existence of being tracked and hunted. Then he said:

> "We'll take this one. We'll gain some space by taking this, this and that out, and we'll put the drawing board over there by the window."

Then, in order to give life and memory to things which were, as yet, still inert, he took me into the bedroom, and in front of the bare mattress, aflame with purple roses on a weft of yellow silk, he said as if uttering some magic spell:

"Now, I'm your man."

As the days passed, the square of windows over the courtyard gained elaborate grilles in arabesques of ironwork, air conditioners, garlands of clothes hung out to dry. I also put my clothes out on the balcony next to his. Shirts, trousers, dresses and socks, all washed in the same water, drying in the same sunshine, merrily proclaiming the adventure of a clear, unequivocal intimacy.

The bell in the elevator stopped working. I often burnt the rice, or served it underdone. He would come straight home from work – after all, that space of his was like a new toy. He ate punctually, took piping hot baths, organized his work, watched the soap opera from Hong Kong on television, went to bed early, and led a life that was as linear as a folktale:

Once upon a time there was a girl whose mother had died and who lived with her three sisters, who were seamstresses... as she was the youngest, her sisters made her run all sorts of errands, delivering work or doing the shopping. One day, her elder sister told her:

> *"Take this doublet to our landlord and on the way back, with the money he gives you, buy half a loaf of bread, and ten cents of tea, for our supper."*

The girl, who was very absent-minded, in order not to forget what she had been told, kept repeating as she walked along:

> *"Half a loaf of bread, ten cents of tea, half a loaf of bread, ten*

cents of tea." On her way back from the landlord's house, distracted by her little ditty, she stumbled as she passed under a beautiful lime tree in blossom, and fell through a mysterious trapdoor. She walked through a labyrinth and eventually came across an enchanted prince who ruled alone among the imposing deserted rooms…

They married and lived happily, until one day, a group of white cranes flew high across the sky… what birds are those, she asked.

"Your father has died," said the prince. "You must go to the funeral. If you don't come back in three days, you will forget me."

"Never," she said. And he:

"Don't make promises!… But you will remember when you see the brier rose on a field of green, for that is my standard!"

Or the other story he told me:

… That night, they became man and wife and, before daybreak, they left taking all their belongings with them. Stopping only to eat, travelling by day and resting by night, they arrived at Quzhou.

"There are five roads leading out of this city. Which one shall we take?" said Cui.
… Then they decided to go to Tanzhou, a city that was very remote from the capital…

"We'll be safe here", said Cui. "We'll be able to live in peace as husband and wife for the rest of our days."

They rented a house in the market area and put a sign above the door, which said: CUI, JADE CARVER. Time passed like a flash. Little more than a year had gone by when Xiuxiu said:

"We are fine here. But my old parents must have suffered hardships since I left them to follow you. Lets send someone to fetch them to come and live with us."

"I'll go," said Cui.

On his way, he met a traveller. The man wore a cloth coat with a white collar, the same colour as his shin guards and sandals, and his face was hidden by a large hat made from bamboo fibre. When they passed each other, the traveller looked at Cui carefully...

As the poet said:

"A naughty child rang the bell loudly
With fluttering wings, the lovebirds flew off".

But in our little Babel, the morning birds chirp inside their cages.

Life revolves around rituals: the porter dragging the rubbish containers out. A nanny comforting a crying baby. The Japanese grandfather bringing the children home from the international school. The haughty young man who takes his precious dogs for a walk. The school kids who swap video games on the steps outside the apartment block. The blonde watering the periwinkle on her balcony. With a background music of clacking mah-jong tablets, a never ending Cantonese opera, the cry of the glutinous rice vendor. On sunny days, a Persian cat would meticulously lick its paws, and the perpetually closed curtains of a mysterious window would billow, the only sign of life being a shaft of light visible through a crack at night.

One sunlit morning, shouts and groans echoed round the

shadowy courtyard. A man's angry voice, that of a woman complaining. As if in some secret pagan order, knives, a clipper, a pair of scissors, skewers fell in a shower of metal from some window, making a noise as they hit the concrete floor.

My lord and master was having his breakfast, and came to the balcony. The bowl of noodles he was carrying seemed to me to be lit up – compared to the colour of his skin, the white of the sky seemed dark and sombre.

"What was that?" I asked.

"Nothing," he replied. "A couple having a quarrel. It's perfectly normal in families." I seemed to catch a shadowy innocence, almost a type of insolence, in his excited look. But at that point a cricket sang up on the S. Januário Road. As if the light of day were blocked by some dark filter, the morning was shrouded in some inexpressible foreboding. My vulnerable world revealed a black star. Unable to imagine what fate lay in store, I nevertheless knew I would one day receive a gift, full of perdition and routine.

As always, what I yearned for was also what I most feared.

Beyond the courtyard there was the city and its incessant toil, ever more fragile and precious, ever more valued and exquisite, like the memories of an old man, or an ancient fragment of silk, its wise and worldly waft undone.

DAYDREAM AT HAC-SÁ

"Excuse me", she would say to the man lying on the blue towel who twiddled his toes in time to an inaudible music. He would take his earphones off and ask:

"Do you need something?" And she would say:

"Yes, would you have a sheet of paper by any chance?"

"What for?" he would ask, intrigued. And she would say:

"To write a poem, of course."

There would be no of course about it. He would sit up, smoothing his towel, and look towards the water's edge where his wife and daughter are playing and paddling, as if asking for help. Grains of grey sand would fall as he stroked his beard, perplexed.

It's a Chinese holiday, the day of the Dragon Boat, and everybody is at the beach. And a family like that one, a model of the utmost normality, shines against the June sky like a jewel: mother and daughter playing in the water, and he, relaxed, enjoying the sun and listening to music, lying on his blue towel on the black sand. And lo and behold, his wife's friend who had come with them, and had remained stuck between the sea and the forest oaks, is asking him for a piece of paper, and no sir, it's not a tissue paper she wants to clean her sunglasses with or wrap her sun cream in, it's a sheet of paper, of all things, to write a poem on.

It's obvious she can't ask for a piece of paper. Besides it's not important, she can write it later. No need to worry. The poem will have soon flown away, but another one will come, they always do, it's part of our perdition, all living things cry out silently, quiver, whisper, murmur, endlessly advertise themselves and say: you live and wonder why we have a voice and a name, and if we have a name it's so that you can call us, and in so doing, you are inevitably weaving threads that entwine and spin the web that sustains you in the air, a world away from the families who play happily, eat and listen to music on the beach at Hac-Sá – Black Sand Beach. She sat down dejectedly, but she was only pretending, for deep down she was enjoying it like a cat stretching. She smoothed down the black straps of her bikini, and lay down on her towel, gazing up at the dark green catkins of the forest oaks, swaying and undulating overhead, like a wreath of delicate lacework.

Boys with dragons tattooed on them passed by, and one of them gave her a discreet smile. She felt dizzy, the moving clouds were being chased by the greenish trunks of the forest oaks. A second dizzy spell, as the crowd of merrymakers ate lychees, grapes, ice creams, grilled chicken thighs, skewered fish balls with curry sauce; systematically spitting onto the sand husks, shiny seeds, sticks, bones, bags, in a veritable orgy of trash disposal.

That's rich! She laughed to herself, she also made trash, verbal trash. Accepting her guilt, she once again stretched idly. Be quiet, her inner voice said, with sudden irritation. There's no paper here. Well, write on the sand then. She turned over, furious. She could perfectly well think of other things. For a few moments she would like to be her friend who was splashing about in the murky water. Just in order to experience the clear, simple, law-abiding order that stitched together thoughts in a head like hers.

Once again, the boys with their smooth, tattooed skin passed by in the opposite direction. Her inner voice fell silent, startled, while on the huge white screen of the sky, black sand, forest oaks, and the forbidden images of a recent past paraded themselves. Not now, she moaned, in distress. Families intrepidly went on eating. Like mechanical birds, parents fed their little children. Lovable, beautiful, those children, with their dark eyes shining like glass beads, skin like magnolia petals, hair like fine dark silk. Their children were beautiful, really beautiful, and she had none. If she was given one, he would call her mother, and what if later on, he wanted one of those dragons tattooed on his chest? She dreamed:

"Mother, I'm going to have a tattoo done on my chest."

"Son, don't do that. You'll be like all the others who have dragons tattooed on their chests, and you'll have to obey the one who's also got a dragon on his back, and a long tale round his hips."

"Mother, I'm already like all those who've got black hair and slanting eyes."

"My son, you're already the same as all those who live and breathe under the Sun."

She hugs her imagined son and kisses his smooth flat chest.

"Hey! You're almost falling off your towel! You've got your

face and mouth covered in black sand. Laughing stridently, her friend shakes gleaming droplets from herself, which have nothing to do with the muddy stretch of water from where they come. Lets go back to Macau, her friend says decisively. It's late and it's going to rain."

The poem about to be born, unembellished and ethereal at that precise moment, without any paper to give body and life to its skeleton of letters, came to her now in the greens and browns of the beach, the smell of warm sand and bodies, the bay as gentle as a womb, the forest oaks brushing the pregnant air with their long verdant fingers. But it wasn't, after all, this that made the moment precious and eternal: it was the words that came to her on the breeze, joined together like bundles of heraldic arrows, harsh words, gentle, or atonic ones, banal murmurings in at least five different languages: sweethearts cooing in Cantonese. Merry Filipino women chatting away in Tagalog with their friends and in English with their little masters building castles out of the black sand. Groups dressed smartly, as if out to see a cheap film, whispering in Mandarin. Portuguese families talking loudly, as if hoisting a flag.

Hail, Mother. She wrote with her finger in the sand, as she got up.

THE LAST SUPPER

Angelica

While the other pupils tired themselves out with their exercises in English, Angelica avoided the watchful eye of the strict teacher, scribbling poems in the margins of exercise books, which she then copied out neatly in her diary, illustrated with baroque angels, hearts, garlands, and theatrical masks. She needed no great intellectual inspiration, but raising her gaze through the glass door, she would look out into the small inner courtyard.

It rains without stopping in the gloomy courtyard
There is no sign of spring on the bare fig tree.
The New Year's lanterns have already faded
Only my memories shine
Like neon roses in the cold afternoon.

I came across the word "neon" in a text the teacher gave us about Macau at night, and I thought it would look good in a poem. I'd like him to see it, but I'd never dare to show him.

The Drama Master

I decided to take a short cut from the staff room to the gymnasium by crossing the recently watered garden. Angelica is following behind, holding up the pale cottons and bright silks and brocades at arm's length, so that they don't brush the wet grass. The gardener lowers the jet of his hosepipe towards the green tuft of banana plants. The small domestic routine of the place had caused a slim gardener like Pan An to divert his hosepipe one April morning, so that Angelica could pass by with her flowing load of costumes for princes, fairies and hobgoblins for that afternoon's performance.

The party sparkled into life in the clean air. The bauhinia cascaded in a mass of rose coloured petals over the azaleas. The pupils were free that morning. The women teachers had gone to the hairdresser, the boys were limbering up on the playing field. Only Angelica had stayed behind, under the pretext of taking the costumes for the play over to the dressing rooms. For a whole year, Angelica had been morose and silent, full of sighs, writing poems, drawing aimlessly, her only confidante being her diary, but thanks to the preparations for the play, to be performed during the school's festival, she had got a new lease of life. She was following me, happy to be of some last minute help. Blinded by raw innocence, scheming to make me fall into springtime's trap.

There was an almost imperceptible rhythmic stirring among the patch of parsley. Angelica contains herself, holding her breath, her young girl's antennae quivering tensely:

> "Sir!" She calls me anxiously, probing the silence. The accomplice of insects and birds, she lowers her voice, whispers, hoarse and decisive:

> "Sir, wait!"

I walk ahead of her, unable to contain my smile, and with genuine indifference I don't look at whatever it is she wants me to see. She walks faster, murmuring into the rustling silks she is carrying:

"Even the little grey kittens make love…"

On the steps up to the gymnasium, which is also used for social occasions, the alternately arranged pots of begonias and geraniums, ranging from the purest white to bright scarlet, form a guard of honour for us. The gardener, proudly coiling his hosepipe, smiles at me triumphantly. With a gentle wave of the hand, I congratulate him for creating such harmony.

Angelica moodily distributes the velvet jackets, pannier dresses, lace fans and wooden swords among the hangers. Each outfit has a name attached to it: Silvia Chan, Paulo Dias, Ana Leong, Viriato, Sara, Anabela, Regina da Luz, João Lei, each name evoking an excited face, blushing with nervousness and expectation, for it is not every day that they take to the stage to perform a play for the School's anniversary, in this case the one hundred and thirteenth.

I leave Angelica to her task, and return to the narrow wardrobe, at the back of the staff room, my ear capturing the sounds of bygone times, while high collared Chinese coats, ball gowns, gloves, hats, sleep in their mothballs. I'm looking for Maria. There's no one around. Past directors look down at me from their solemn portraits. We always knew nothing lasts forever, their dark eyes seem to say.

I cross the tiny coffee lounge, the dark corridor smells of fresh polish, and as I arrive in the hall, transformed by the magical brightness of the midday sun, I see the domestic staff, in festive mood, laying the huge T shaped table with white cloths.

I summon up my memory so that I can record what I see. I want to remember this forever. I repeat: they lay white cloths over the long table! The tone of my voice awakens an echo that no other part of the world returns as it does here.

Returning Dona Emiliana's cheerful greetings as she bustles around giving orders and advice, I pause for a moment and lean against the glass of one of the inner courtyards, a tiny universe of birds, toads, dragonflies, purple lilies and prowling cats.

"Oh! Dona Emiliana, I'm beginning to feel hungry."

"Make the most of it. Who knows? Maybe it's the last one."

In the courtyard, the barren fig tree is adorned with new shoots, as green as pure jade.

It's foolish to love a place. A space enclosed by tiled walls, which jealously guards like a treasure its games of light and shadow, its routine of lessons and playtime, removed from the noise of urban life.

"It's foolish to love a place that no longer exists!" I say sorrowfully, sure that Dona Emiliana will understand me. But Dona Emiliana didn't hear me. Her careful little steps have already taken her into the library.

Angelica

In the darkness of the garden the children chase each other, breathless, shrieking like swallows. The little girls trail the bows of their parties dresses behind them, the boys tread on their undone shoelaces. The grown-ups fill the great hall, but the gentle ripple of conversation and laughter doesn't cover the throbbing rhythm of the school's traditional combo, the 'Tuna', which plays continuously, switching without pause from "Brown Eyes" to "The Boy on the Flying Trapeze". Plate in hand, many find it difficult to know what to choose. Some methodically try a bit of everything: hot pot, bean stew, special full rice, *adêcabidela*, *bafassá* pork, split-back prawn, crab and papaya flower, salt cod chutney... Eating has nothing to do with the sin of gluttony, but with a deeply felt melancholy. Those who manage to resist the tamarind and shrimp paste pork, with its heavy rice, the *capela* pork, the delicious turnip *bebinca*, allow themselves to be tempted by the *apa-bico*, the little tarts and deep-fried meat patties, and then are irredeemably bewitched by the desserts, sweet potato *bebinca*, *baji* cake, mango pudding, caramel custard, China slices, *menino* cake, the countless, tempting secrets of old aunties and grannies.

During this time, Angelica sighed disconsolately as she sat at the end of the bench under the bauhinia. Beyond the large glass doors, both of which were open, she could see the party in full swing, elegant ladies eating and chatting, the men glass in hand, all devotedly taking part in some ritual of atonement.

She watched the drama master wandering, with his long legged gait, among the groups of partygoers, followed by a pack of little pages and pixies, their mouths smudged with sweets over the remains of their make-up.

> "And he doesn't even look this way..." she sighed again. Suddenly, she sees her mother walk up to him, her crimson lips smiling broadly, her generous figure corseted inside her purple satin dress.

> "You look like a Holy Week procession, Leopoldina," she thought. But then she changed her mind contritely, upon seeing the bishop's white habit in the vicinity:

"God forgive me, I meant a carnival parade."

She shifted her position, and pulled down her dark blue velvet skirt in an attempt to cover her solitary adolescent's large thighs. Her mother was guffawing, laughing with her beloved teacher, while her heaving bosom caused her necklace to glitter. Unaware of this, he swept back his long blond hair. The children rushed around, knocking back Coca-Cola out of paper cups.

The Director, still deep in conversation with the Bishop, looked concerned. Could it be that he saw her and thought her skirt too short? The Director was so kind and fair, and never got on the pupils' nerves. But of course, he doesn't want his authority abused! She said this out loud, as she pulled down her skirt. The 'Tuna' was now playing "The Black Ship", and Angelica plunged her round white fingers into her hair, absorbed in the voluptuous pain of a first, impossible love. She wanted so much to be happy, daring and experienced like her mother. Her body was a replica of her mother's, but devoid of her tenacity and pagan joyfulness, it seemed soft and limp, like a badly executed drawing. All of a sudden, jumping up in response to an unexpected fit of inspiration, she rushed towards the party and into the light of the room.

"I'm not going to let you have him all to yourself!" She leapt up the stairs, angry, shaking her vast young hips, and fanning her burning cheeks with her little purse.

The bauhinia

The following day, the silence was stitched together from the tattered memories of the party. In the mid-morning break, the pupils queued up in the canteen to buy lemon tea, fried pork rolls, soya milk. The more energetic ones rushed off towards the playing fields, while those who understood written Chinese read out stories from magazines about singers and film stars from Hong Kong to their illiterate friends. Angelica went to her favourite seat carrying her snack and her diary under her arm. She stopped suddenly at the edge of the lawn, puzzled. She was used to answering her own questions, but on this occasion she feverishly searched for an answer to the unexpected sight that met her.

During all her five long years at the school, one thousand two hundred and eighty days not counting Sundays and public holidays, more than a thousand days woven with a thousand experiences, she had never seen the director give an unjust or unwise order. So what she saw was not a whim of the board of governors. The school continued as it always had, with teachers from Macau and others from Portugal, some pupils who studied diligently while others fooled around as if that was all there was to life; the play had been a success, and many had shed a tear, not because they were watching high drama, but because of the talent and dedication shown by all involved in the performance. It was therefore highly improbable that what was being done to the little tree was due to some bad feng shui.

She gave up trying to understand, and with her heart twisted in pain, and her dry eyes on the verge of a flood of tears, Angelica stood watching:

With an old electric saw, the princely gardener, as always impassive, was methodically cutting its branches, severing its trunk, killing the beautiful bauhinia in full flower.

Books Published by Gávea-Brown

Portuguese Studies
Onésimo T. Almeida, ed., *José Rodrigues Miguéis – Lisbon in Manhattan*
Francisco C. Fagundes, *A Poet's Way With Music: Humanism in Jorge de Sena's Poetry*
Francisco C. Fagundes, ed., *Ecos de Uma Viagem: Em honra de Eduardo Mayone Dias*
George Monteiro, ed., *The Man Who Never Was: Essays on Fernando Pessoa*
Nelson H. Vieira, ed., *Roads to Today's Portugal*

Portuguese American Studies
Sam Beck, *Manny Almeida's Ringside Lounge*
Richard Beale Davis, *The Abbé Corrêa In America, 1812-1820*. Pref. by Gordon S. Wood. Afterword by Léon Boudon
Maria A. Duarte and Ronald W. Sousa, *Reading the Harper: On a Portuguese Immigrant Poem from California, 1901*

Poetry
Onésimo T. Almeida, ed., *The Sea Within – A Selection of Azorean Poetry*. Trans. by George Monteiro
Eugénio de Andrade, *The Shadow's Weight*. Trans. by Alexis Levitin
Thomas J. Braga, *Portingales*
Emanuel Felix, *The Possible Journey, Poetry (1965-1992)*. Trans. by John M. Kinsella
José Martins Garcia, *Temporal*
João Teixeira de Medeiros, *Do Tempo e de Mim*. Ed. by Onésimo T. Almeida
George Monteiro, *The Coffee Exchange*
Fernando Pessoa, *Self-Analysis and Thirty Other Poem*. Trans. by George Monteiro
Jorge de Sena, *In Crete with the Minotaur and Other Poems*. Trans. by George Monteiro

Fiction
Camilo Castelo Branco, *Doomed Love (a family memoir)*. Trans. by Alice R. Clemente
Visions of China: Stories from Macau. Various authors. Trans. by David Brookshaw
Alice R. Clemente, ed., *Sweet Marmalade, Sour Oranges: Contemporary Portuguese Women's Fiction*. Various translators.
Vitorino Nemésio, *Stormy Isles: An Azorean Tale*. Trans. by Francisco C. Fagundes
Dias de Melo, *Dark Stones*. Trans. by Gregory McNab
José Rodrigues Miguéis, *Steerage and Ten Other Stories*. Ed. by George Monteiro. Various translators

Theater
Bernardo Santareno, *The Judgment of Father Martinho – A Dramatic Narrative in Two Acts*. Trans. by Celso de Oliveira
Bernardo Santareno, *The Promise*. Trans. by Nelson H. Vieira

Autobiography
Francisco C. Fagundes, *Hard Knocks: An Azorean-American Odyssey*